# *SPELL CASTING*

Edited by

Claire Savage

First published in Great Britain in 2001 by
*POETRY NOW*
Remus House,
Coltsfoot Drive,
Peterborough, PE2 9JX
Telephone  (01733) 898101
Fax (01733) 313524

*Copyright Contributors 2001*

HB ISBN 0 75432 654 3
SB ISBN 0 75432 655 1

# FOREWORD

'Brevity is the soul of wit'

A poet can say in thirty lines what it takes a novelist to say in 200 pages, is a comment that has been bandied about for centuries. The ability to express an emotion or describe a momentous event in a few lines has shown a facility for language, a vocabulary to be envied and an ear for the music of words. All qualities associated with the finest poets.

What about writers of prose? Surely those of us that find pleasure in prose still possess all of the skills mentioned above? With this in mind we decided to put our prose writers to the test and created a new challenge using the 'snapper', a 250 word short story.

The spine chiller seemed to be the perfect place to start. What a test of skills this would be. Could our writers send a shiver down our spines in 250 words or less? As you will read, they rose to the challenge and have proved that once the imagination has been engaged and a picture formed in the mind, the skilled writer of prose can create a fully rounded world in few words.

# CONTENTS

## PRINCESS SNOW WHITE

Following the overthrow of the Royal Family, the young Princess Snow White had dragged herself across the country to Wales. Falling asleep on a small hill she was so exhausted.

In the morning, seven miners on their way to work found her. They carried her back to their small cottage. She told them of the Army coming for her family - and how her wicked stepmother, the queen, had tried to poison her.

The miners told her they would protect and take care of her.

On the day after, she was alone and after the seven miners had left for work. Their ghetto-blasters covered up the sound of the Royal helicopter. Dressed up like some old gypsy, the old queen crept up to the little wooden cottage. She gave Snow White a nice red apple to eat. Instead of throwing her into a deathly coma, she just fainted and when the miners came home they were upset.

Taking their picks they sent word to other miners to march on the London Palace and put Snow White on the throne. Thousands of men came and marched behind the seven leaders. Then they threw the old queen in the Tower.

Snow White made the seven into Lords and Wales became the new British *capital.*

*Colin Allsop*

## LUCK AT LAST FOR MISS MUFFET AND HER FAMILY

'Muffet! Will you stop grumbling; we can only afford curds and whey for each meal, every day.'

'I find it sickening too!' Complained Muffet's father; who was a very lazy man who didn't really try to get a job!

'And I'm sick of the pair of you! Go and eat your curds and whey in the garden, Muffet!

Which was rather unfair on Muffet, she did *try* to be as good as she could!

Muffet hadn't sat long on her little tuffet, when something very thin and light landed on her hand; it seemed like something alive with a lot of legs.

'Ooh, go away!' she shouted and started to run.

'Hey!' said a very thin voice: 'Don't run away from *me!* I'm a *lucky* spider!'

Then as Muffet returned to her tuffet, she saw the tiny creature had very small eyes, and a small mouth, and he seemed to be smiling at her; Muffet smiled back, but said rather sadly:

'You can't give us human money, and we're very poor! We only have curds and whey to eat at each meal!'

'I can take you for a splendid meal in Spido-land: Of course, we have different food from humans, but when I touch a white coloured leaf, I can make anything appear at all, even big human tasty meals!'

'But would you have time to make that appear *every* day, and for daddy and mummy too?'

'I will make some money appear that you can take home to your daddy and mummy.' Spinny Spider started to say, but Muffet interrupted him: 'They'll think I've stolen it!'

'No they won't! I'll write a little message for you to give them as well.'

'How can you write?' asked Muffet, very puzzled.

'I get a very thin little twig,' replied Spinny: 'Wrap a leaf round it, leaving a little bit of black twig showing, and make that come to a point, then I write with that.'

'Let me see you write, please,' asked Muffet.

This was Spinny Spider's message:

'This is some money I'm leaving you, which will last you several weeks for buying good food, and when you are needing some more, Muffet must come to my tree in the garden, where I have my web, and my magic leaf, to tell me that you're ready for more.'

> Best wishes
>
> Spinny Spider

When Muffet went indoors again, *with* a clean dish, Spinny must have magiced that clean!

Her mother demanded 'Where have you been? What's in you hand?'
'It's notes and notes of money!' exclaimed her father.
'Please read this note from Spinny Spider,' Muffet urged.
'Who?' exclaimed both of her parents.
But as Muffet's mother looked at the writing, she remarked
'Well that certainly doesn't look like human writing!'
'It isn't! It isn't!' Muffet started to shout, 'Spinny *is* a spider; a *lucky* spider!'
Then she explained to her parents how Spinny created his magic.

Her father was feeling the notes,
'They *are* real!' he exclaimed.
'Have you thanked Spinny?' asked her mother, beginning to believe Muffet now, but still feeling a little bewildered.
'Oh, of course Mum. Do you want to thank him too? He'll be in his tree outside.'
'Come on Fred, we will go and thank him too. We should have much happier days from now on!'

Another surprising thing that must have been more of Spinny's magic, the following day Muffet's father suddenly had a strong urge to try and apply for a gardening job!

*Marjorie Cowan*

## 'ERBERT HARMSTRONG

Once upon a time . . . there was a wolf called 'Erbert.

He was 'Erbert W. But . . . nobody knew for sure what the 'W' stood for.

He'd just added it himself - a bit of a filler - to cover up a wisecrack, that was plainly too close to the truth . . .

'Erbert was a special kind of wolf. We've all heard of a double agent. Well, 'Erbert was a double wolf.

He owned a circus which gave performance worldwide. The most astounding acrobat feats; men turned into pigs; and clowns everywhere. 'Erbert loved to dress up as a sheep and shout (my, how he would shout!).

'Wolf, Wolf!' he shouted. 'Watch out, watch out! There's a wolf about. You mustn't go to any other circus but mine. Mine is the only circus that protects you from the wolf.'

Now most of the world thought that 'Erbert's circus was a rip-off. That he charged far, far too much to access his show. But 'Erbert did have a few tricks that were entirely original, up his sleeve.

Every tree is known by his own fruit. In a thicket, in a wood (let it now be understood), there grew an elm. But with 'Erbert at the helm, it was no good.

The strange thing about 'Erbert's circus was that once you were admitted (to see one of his shows), it was impossible to see the real 'Erbert or any of the other performers. They had the power to transform themselves. You see, 'Erbert could never, never ever be wrong. No, not even for a moment. 'Erbert was always right. He was a right 'Erbert.

Throughout the decades, many many people became fascinated with 'Erbert and his circus. They faithfully sacrificed for it, to keep it 'on the road' - that is until they realised that it was 'Erbert who was the wicked wolf all along. He was that rum ringmaster, that caused many a disaster.

'Erbert's fruit was 'strongly 'armful' as one may say in Brum -

He was a wolf in sheep's clothing who cried out to people to 'Watch out for the wolf . . . '

*Peter N Griffiths*

## A FAIRY TALE

Oberon's castle lay fair and square in the land of Magick.

Her throne of gold lay in the centre of the courtyard, while fairy attendants saw to her every need, even to protecting her with a range of cannon, armoury, and a portcullis, and moat.

Yet all was not well in her land of Magick. Her Chief Wizard Grimmshaw, was envious of Oberon's position, as it was obvious the Chief Wizard desired the adoration fawned upon Oberon by her fairy worshippers, who adored her tremendously.

Grimmshaw set out to undermine Oberon, by telling those who followed her that she was a deceitful queen who despised them.

The faithful fairies told Oberon, who sent for the wicked and evil, Chief Wizard.

'Grimmshaw' she said as he knelt at her feet.
'Grimmshaw' she repeated 'you are my Chief Wizard, and I look to you to protect not only me, but all the fairies, and even Magickland itself, why then, do you deceive me?'

Grimmshaw lay at her feet and sobbed, for he had been found out, and it was in Oberon's power to banish him from Magickland to the Outerlands.

'I know not why my Lady Queen' Grimmshaw admitted 'I ask you to be merciful to me.'

Oberon placed her hand gently upon the head of her Chief Wizard.

'Your task' she told him 'is to allocate each fairy a flower to personally protect and become responsible for, will you do that for me?'
'Yes, your Majesty' he agreed.

And so it is, that even today, each garden flower has its own fairy power, who is exactly the same colour as the flower it protects.

And because of her wisdom, Grimmshaw became the most devoted follower of Oberon, and every garden in the world owes a huge vote of thanks to Oberon, the Queen of the Fairies . . .

*Gordon Bannister*

## LITTLE BO-PEEP

Had she really lost her sheep
This young girl?
Should she really leave them alone?

She had felt alone so often on the
cold hillside herself.
'Alone and palely loitering
Though sedge is withered from
the lake
And no birds sing.'

So she doesn't know where to find
them - perhaps watching some far
off star with the Magi
out of time and place

'Peep' indeed, now I see you
now I don't, but you're always
there . . . probably Peep-Bo Peep-Bo . . .
There was a time and this was
it, when they would be gone as she
opened her eyes.

The frisson descended into fear
They had left her alone. Who was
looking after who now?

Will they come to find her
will they miss each other if she moves
away or will she miss them if
she doesn't?

Sure they may find their way home
but where was that and did she
live there?

Little girl without a name, shepherd
in a man's world wandering the
boundaries and lost to settlement's law
and safety. Now you will be an alien of aliens,
nameless one.

Shall we call you Mary, you
deserve a name, or Josephine what
name would you like?

Across the skyline a tall young man
with a crook drove her beloved
sheep towards her - she was found
again and in her fear had found
a name.

Little Bo-Peep had found her sheep
and herself.

She felt she was home at last
no need to play peep-bo. Her eyes
were opened as she took in the
tall stranger and her sheep
coming homeward

*James O'Grady*

## THREE LITTLE LADS

The three youngsters wedged the cardboard washing machine boxes side by side in the alley. They lined them with newspapers and settled into their great-coats for sleep.

'Night then, I'll give you a call in the morning with early tea and the Sundays,' said Mick sarcastically. They had barely nodded off when the steady tread of a bobby on the beat roused them.

'Sorry lads - you can't doss down here - this is a fire exit, so needs to be kept clear.' They gathered their meagre possessions together and trailed off.

Jem cautiously negotiated the broken window and dropped into the vacant warehouse, beckoning his companions to follow. Settling again, they couldn't believe their bad luck when a torch's beam disturbed them and a burly watchman's face glared down at them.

'This place is being demolished first thing in the morning, been condemned for years - get out of it!'

They plodded wearily out of town until straw bales in a harvested field were silhouetted against the first rays of dawn.

'It'll take a bit of huffin' and puffin' to blow this lot down,' said Jem hauling the last bale into position.
'They're using straw to build proper houses now, you know - so this should shelter us for one night, at least.

The three lads snuggled contentedly into their sweet-smelling den as the rain settled in for the day.

*Kirsty M Adlard*

# GOLDILOCKS AND THE THREE BEARS

There was once a very pretty little girl. Everyone called her Goldilocks because of her long golden hair which hung to her shoulders in ringlets.

Because she was so pretty, everyone gave her cakes and chocolates and sweets and soon she became very fat and not so pretty. She could not stop eating and she was so heavy that she broke every piece of furniture that she sat on.

Her parents put her in a cottage of her own and soon she broke all the furniture there too.

A family came to live next door. Father Bear was a carpenter, Mother Bear a doctor and Baby Bear grew up to be very handsome.

The family befriended Goldilocks and Father Bear soon made her some new furniture which was strong enough for her to sit on without breaking it.

Mother Bear recommended a special diet for her, and showed her how to eat sensibly and cook nutritious meals to maintain her weight and figure.

Goldilocks soon lost her weight and became beautiful again.

Baby Bear had been away at college and when he came back after graduating, he saw Goldilocks as he had never seen her before, and fell in love with her. He asked her to marry him and they had a big wedding and invited all the villagers to come and join the celebrations.

It was the wedding of the year and one which was talked about in the village ever after.

*Gwendoline Bennett*

## ONCE UPON A TIME

Cindy was cheesed off. She could murder a cuppa and Dert and Gaisy were too busy playing GloomFader. 'Ugly gits!' Cindy thought.

Just then Roy the Posty rang.

'Hi Babe. Doing anything tonight? Got a groovy do here.'

She was just about to take the invite when Dert and Gaisy grabbed it.

'Ooh! Dig that!' they wheezed. 'Best bib and tuckers night! Get ironing sis.'

Cindy was feeling sorry for herself. They'd belted off with the invite and left her holding the baby. Butch slipped his arm round her.

'Chin up kid. I love you.'
'I wanna go,' Cindy moaned. 'I ain't got nuttin' to wear and no fare to get there.'
'Hold on,' Butch said, 'won't be a mo!'

A few minutes later an old gypsy hag banged.
'Cross my palm with silver, luvvie.'
'Fat chance,' Cindy yelled.

Suddenly she was dressed in the latest fab gear and designer trainers. Her hand held a fiver!

Cindy went in a black cab. The party was a wow, with a hunk called Prin spreading himself around. He couldn't get enough of Cindy. They danced the salsa for hours. The '12 o'clock Rag' proved too much and exhausted Cindy made a quick exit.

The next day Prin came with one of her trainers. Everyone claimed it. Prin knew, by the smell, it belonged to Cindy.

That was how that gal met her Prin.

Charming story! But that gypsy did look a tad like Butch in drag though.

*Aleene Hatchard*

## PRINCESS POPPY AND THE FROG PRINCE

This is not so much a fairy story as a furry tale - even a cat
tail. For this is about the pretty Princess Poppy, her son Billy and a
search for the real Frog Prince.

A petite tabby pussy cat, Poppy was also a young single mother.
She began life in rather a Cinderella kind of way. Evicted from two
homes in a row, Poppy and Billy ended up in a Cats' Rescue Home
where, chosen from all the rest, they were whisked away. In her new
home, Poppy was now nicknamed 'Princess' and treated royally.
However, there was just one thing missing - the handsome prince.

Now, in Poppy and Billy's new home, two more cats soon arrived
- Rupert and Wilfred; pages in her book of life. Or at least, good frog-
catchers who, along with Billy (who rather fancied the idea of a new
dad), would bring home frogs. Far and wide they searched, returning
with froggies of all shapes and sizes. Great big ones, little squiddly ones
- even rather vocal ones that squealed a lot and hopped rapidly away.
Poppy kissed them all. Some needed a second kiss - this time a kiss of
life - to revive them after the shock.

Eventually, Billy brought home a whopper hopper. Just one kiss
and - *shazam!* No, not a genie but a puff of smoke and a monarch
amongst moggies standing before her.

Needless to say, they lived 'hoppily' ever after!

*Geraldine Laker*

## MODERN DAY FAIRY TALE

'Do you think this new dress makes me look fat?'
Hansel glared at his sister who had been complaining all day about
being hungry. She really was getting on his wick.
'Gretel, the dress is fine. It's your great big wobbly belly and bum that
makes you look fat. Now come on, if we are to make the enchanted
cottage, eat the cakes, and get home before dark. This forest is spooked
you know,' said Hansel, scaring the wits out of his sister, already tearful
at his cruel 'fat' jibe - the result of one too many cake-eating trips.

'Look Hansel, the enchanted cottage!' exclaimed Gretel. She never tired
of seeing the delicious house.
Reaching the cottage they began greedily stuffing themselves.
Suddenly, as they were tucking into the front door, it swung open.
'Not you two brats again,' said the ugly old hag, grabbing them. 'Brat
pies!'
But before she could push them into the oven, they stamped on her feet
and then they pushed her in the oven.
'Janie, are you ready for our date?' An ugly old man stood at the door.
'Hello,' he said to them 'is she ready yet?'
'She will be in about 10 minutes,' said Hansel. Both giggling, they ran
home.

*Irene Battle*

## Out On The Razzle

Rapunzel stood at the window of her 9th floor flat in South East London. Where was that no good . . . Sonofabitch. She looked towards Woolwich Arsenal just as a battered Robin Reliant spluttered into view. Dermot prised himself out of the three-wheeler and peered up to where his beautiful Razzle was framed in the window.

'I am being held prisoner against my will' screamed Rapunzel, adding 'and where the 'ell 'have you bin?'
Dermot yelled something unchivalrous about the South Circular before stating boldly that he would soon whisk her away into the night - to the rave-up in Hither Green.
'I suppose my lord 'as a cunning plan' shouted Rapunzel sarcastically, 'but if it's about letting me long silken tresses down - forget it!'
'Oh' said Dermot disappointedly, 'well what about the knotted bedsheets?'
'Dermot' shouted Rapunzel patiently, 'I am wearing a mini, stilettos and designer tights - and you want me to abseil down nine storeys using a pair of winceyette sheets . . . !'
Dermot was nothing if not persistent. As darkness fell, he squinted up towards that small aperture high in the sky. Suddenly he yelled 'Eureka! Me mate Pete the Pane's extending window-cleaning ladders - 'e's told me I can use 'em any time. Don't worry Raz me ol' Dutch - we'll 'ave yer out of yer gilded cage in a jiffy!'
Just then Dermot felt a tug at his sleeve.
'Come on' said Rapunzel, 'the council's been and fixed the lift - where's this bleedin' rave-up?'

*Peter Davies*

## GREEDY GOLDILOCKS

Goldilocks' such a little girl,
Long ringlets and just one tight curl
In the centre of her forehead
Just cross her once and you'll be dead!

This cheerful child could charm her teachers. Her parents portrayed her as patience personified. Yet to her closest confidante, Silvier Shoesmith, she was something else.

She wandered away one Wednesday and saw a family of bears picnicking peacefully near a pond. Desperate to join them, she was disappointed to read a nearby sign:

*By invitation only*
*Granny and Grandad's*
*Golden anniversary*

Goldilocks looked longingly at the honey-glazed hams, spread out on the chequered cloth. She was licking her lips when her gaze landed on the honey nut cereal bars. Lingering behind a larch, hankering after honey and lemon drinks, she plotted her punitive plan.

Refuse my friendship and you'll find
Your furry bodies I will grind
Into a pulp with just one look
You won't read that in any book.

Gazing at the gathering, greed engulfed Goldilocks. Her gaze gradually grew into a glare, generating a golden glow. Each bear became glued to the ground!

Tiptoeing amongst the statuesque creatures, she positioned herself at the picnic edge and filled herself full of food.

Greedy Goldilocks fed her face
At a really alarming pace
Then at once as if on cue
Three brave bears rallied a rescue.

Rupert, Sooty and Paddington Bear
Stood in amazement, fixed a stare
But their rescue came too late
Goldilocks glued them to a gate.

*Catherine Craft*

## THE CRAFTY TROLL

Once upon a time a troll lived in Elfoke forest. Nobody but he in the whole land could spin straw into gold. Three times he spun three rooms full for a miller's beautiful daughter, who later married the king. Twice she paid the troll with jewellery, but the third time she had none left. 'Ah!' said the crafty troll. 'Look ma'am, you ain't getting off that easily. When you have a baby I'll take it away unless you guess my name.' Then off he drove in his trollmobile - *brmm, brmm!*

However, after the baby was born, no way could the queen guess the troll's name when twice he drove to the palace to enquire. Kevin, Nick, Barry and many more names she mentioned, but the troll laughing like a creaking gate, said spitefully 'You've only one day left, and I'll fetch the baby unless you can guess my name.'

Next morning a police goblin on his beat, saw the troll near the road dancing and singing -
  'Everything is okey-doke
  Because I am a clever bloke.'

'Hello sir!' said the police goblin, 'Is this your vehicle standing near the curb?'
'Yes,' the troll muttered.
'Your name sir?'
'Rumpelstiltskin.' (Oh dear, it slipped out without his thinking.)
'Licence, Mr Rumpelstiltskin?'
The troll had no licence. The trollmobile was stolen.

The queen soon heard the news and was so relieved to be able to keep her baby. As for Rumpelstiltskin, he was taken to court because of his crimes, and was imprisoned for life.

*Loré Föst*

## To Sleep Perchance To Dream

She did not want to be here and on her birthday as well, showing support for a landmark was not her idea of a good time.

Still, she was a minor Royal and had to show willing, plus she was going shopping after, then meeting the girls for dinner and a club.

This old hag approaching her, going on because she hadn't been invited or something, surely there were creams available or plastic surgery.

She didn't want someone so ugly near her. She would never let herself go like that.

Ouch! She suddenly felt tired. The whole building was wavering. She would have to lie down . . .


. . . He dematerialised in front of what looked like a giant tent with a Ferris wheel behind it. The place was covered with growth and cobwebs.

'No wonder everyone has fallen asleep,' he thought.

Picking his way over the prone bodies he entered the Dome. There was the most beautiful girl he had ever seen. Without thinking he kissed her. Her eyes opened. Others began to stir.

'You're enchanting,' he said.

'Must have been some sort of spell,' she said.

'Come back to my planet, we'll marry and live happily ever after, he said.

'Sounds like fun. You do have the shopping channel though,' she added.

*Melanie M Burgess*

## SILPHANIA AND LEWIS'S NEW SCHOOL

Silphania was a special fairy. Her job was seeking out unhappy
children, and cheering them up. Hearing a child crying in his bedroom,
she changed her shape to that of a Robin Redbreast. Landing on the
window ledge she pecked the glass. Inside four-year-old Lewis stopped
crying. Drawing back the curtain he was surprised to see the little bird.
Opening the window he let the bird in.

'Hello Lewis, why are you crying?'

Lewis jumped with surprise.

'You talked! Birds can't talk,' he stammered.

'I'm not really a bird, I'm a fairy named Silphania, but I didn't want to
frighten you. Shall I change back to my proper self?'

'Oh yes please.'

With a puff of mist Silphania appeared on his bed.

'Now, why were you crying?'

'I'm starting school tomorrow and I'm afraid, as I will not know
anybody,' Lewis wailed.

'Don't cry, the other children will love you, shall I come with you?'

'Yes please. But what will the other children say when they see a fairy
with me?'

'I'll change myself into a dog so no one will know,' she said.

In the morning a golden retriever bounded up to him and walked beside
him. At the school Lewis hugged the dog and whispered,

'Thank you Silphania,' then kissing his mother, ran happily into the school yard to play.

Lewis's mother turned to find the dog gone.

'That's strange' she thought.

She didn't see the robin whistling happily on the fence.

***Don Woods***

## TRIP TO DOOM

Once upon a time on the tiny planet Spyra, Dragona the magic witch lived alone, her needs met at her commands, at all times.

Dragona was weird, only two feet high. A tiny head, with huge staring eyes, topped a scaly one-armed body. She was web-footed. Her tiny hand had only one finger, green in colour. Her only beauty was a long multicoloured ponytail. She decided on a visit to another planet.

'Acko-na-ki,' she commanded. Immediately a sleek silver spacecraft appeared. Dragona sat at the controls and set off on her journey, she was very excited. She landed on the planet Earth on grassy land, at dusk, all was calm and quiet. About to go exploring, she saw a white creature coming towards her craft. It had four legs and a tail. Soon it was rubbing its back at the craft's door. Full of curiosity and caution too, Dragona opened the door and the creature's pretty face stared at her.

Dragona put her finger out to touch the beautiful creature, a cat called Efritak, who became agitated. He snarled, spat then clawed her finger viciously. Dragona's magic was in her blood now flowing from the wounds, while Efritak ran away like a 'bat out of Hell', eager to hide from the horrible witch.

Dragona's body was soon bloodless. Its magic gone, all that was left of the witch's visit was a strip of scaly skin and a bit of metal. A man passing by picked up the bit of skin and . . . was never seen again.

Efritak never left the safety of his home again.

*Marguerite M Porthouse*

## THE COLLECTOR

'There's power in names . . .' Granny once muttered, 'and The Collector loves power!'

By the light of the street lamp Aine penned a hasty response to a graffiti-query posed by one of the boys.

Pleased, she stood by and admired her handiwork. As a final touch she printed her name on a previously untouched section of the wooden fence, frowning as the orange-tinted light flickered - as if disapproving.

Bored now, and not feeling like going home - all her parents did was drink beer, smoke dope, and microwave TV dinners - she paced the fence, examining each past message and rude drawing; rebelling against the deep hurt she felt way down inside.

Out of the corner of her eye she noticed something change, something odd. She turned as one of her boyfriend Dee's scrawls faded . . . then another . . . and another. Soon there was nothing left but the places where he had printed his name - large and ugly. These too began to fade.

She nearly jumped out of her skin when a rending scream accompanied the disappearance of the first painted signature. She backed up against the lamp as a darkness crept nearer with each following scream.

Finally, when nothing remained to show where Dee had been, there was a dreadful silence and she knew, knew in her bones, that he really was gone.

Aine couldn't think straight enough to run, not even when her own scribbles began to disappear.

*Perry McDaid*

## THE MAGIC BEANS

Once upon a time there lived a young lad called Jason. One day, while walking in the forest, he heard a shrill cry for help. Peering through the bushes, he saw a dwarf up to his waist in mud, struggling in a pool. It was the work of a moment for Jason to undo his belt, throw one end to the dwarf, and pull the little fellow free.

The dwarf, who was a tourist from Brazil, was very grateful to Jason, and gave him a large bag of magic beans.

Jason went happily on his way, until he heard a loud coughing coming from an enormous stone fortress. Peering inside, Jason saw a giant sitting at a table with a handkerchief pressed to his face, suffering from a severe cold.

The giant was a friendly fellow, and invited Jason to come in and have a cup of hot water with him. He said his name was Fortnam (because he lived in a fortress).

'Excuse me,' said Jason, 'but do you really like to drink hot water?'

'I hate the stuff' roared the giant, crashing his huge fist on the table, crushing the beans, some of which flew into his cup. The water turned brown, and gingerly tasting it, the giant declared it to be delicious.

'We will market it together,' he declared.

'Let's call it 'Coughee,' Jason suggested, as you were coughing when we discovered it.

The business prospered, and their shop still exists today, called 'Fortman and Jason'.

*Roy Le Grice*

## LUCY LOCKS

Once upon a time there lived a girl named Lucy Locks. Locks was not her surname, but a nickname she had been given because she could open anything with a lock.

This girl had a bad reputation.

Down at the local Police Station, Lucy was a regular. She had a long line of convictions that no one could punish, because Lucy was too young. The law said she was still a child. The most anyone could do was to caution her. A licence to steal.

A new family had just moved into Lucy's street. Judging by the clothes they wore, and the size of the family car the Bears were well-to-do. That made Lucy Locks think.

One week after the Bears moved in Lucy Locks decided to visit. The Bears were out of course. Lucy Locks climbed in through an open window. It could not be easier.

First Lucy raided the fridge leaving the kitchen looking like a war zone. Then she watched television. All of this activity left Lucy feeling tired. She decided to lie down for a while.

When the Bears returned home and saw the mess in the kitchen they were very angry.

'What a cheek!' Mr Bear exclaimed.

He rushed upstairs where Lucy was still asleep.

'Get out!' Mr Bear screamed.

Lucy Locks rushed out of the house swearing never to steal again.

*Michael Challis*

## Fairy Tale

She came and took me to her world.
Her long flowing hair sparkled with dew like diamonds.
I saw little fairies dance on the water lilies and the foxgloves were like
trees that hung overhead.
The little fairies were born out of sunflower seeds, and she sang a
lullaby.

'Little babies so sweet let the sun shine on you
Give you a heart full of love
May your wings flutter
And your mind grow
And may love follow you wherever you go.'

*Sylvia Morrow*

## SYLVESTER'S NEW SHOES

Once upon a time there was a very spoilt young man. Sylvester had anything he wanted but he always wanted more. Now he craved the smartest pair of shoes in the new shoe shop just off the main street.

The manager called his assistant. Sylvester stared at her. Despite her shabby clothes, she was the most beautiful girl he had ever seen. He agreed with her the shoes she found were smart but he thought the sparkling buckles were odd.

'They are meant for any occasion,' said the manager. 'But you must never get them dirty. Look after them and they'll serve you well.'

Sylvester gazed at the girl. 'Will you come to a dance at my home tomorrow?'

She smiled. 'I'd love to!' she replied.

At the dance, he waltzed away the night with her. Later, they walked in the moonlit garden after heavy rain. She stumbled beside a rose bed and he lurched into mud and thorns which soiled and scratched his new shoes. At once, the enchantment of the night turned ugly. Thunder roared, lightning flashed, he heard a cackle of laughter. His tender glance at her became one of horror. His beautiful girl had changed into an evil old hag.

'Spoilt you are, spoiled you'll remain!' she cried. 'Those shoes won't let you enjoy life again!'

And so it proved. Everything he touched or saw was shabby and grotesque. Neither could he take off the shoes. His life was indeed spoiled for ever after.

*Barbara Carpenter*

# THE WAKING BEAUTY

Once upon a time . . .

. . . in the land they called Happenstance, there lived a king and queen who were very much in love. And at long last came a little baby princess to make their joy complete.

Being a busy couple, the monarchs had to advertise for a nanny. They interviewed many candidates, including one smelly old crone who swore vengeance when she was passed over.

The woman returned in disguise on the princess's sixteenth birthday, bringing with her 'a gift' of a stereo system. Little did the king and queen realise, when they gave the present to their daughter, that it was enchanted, and that when she went to play a record on the turntable she would prick herself on its needle.

From that day forward no one in the castle could sleep a wink. The staff wandered the halls at night, the king and queen rowed all the time over the smallest of things, and the princess herself gradually descended into a kind of sleep-deprived madness . . .

Well, a charming young prince eventually heard about this situation and travelled to the castle to see if he could help. He found it populated by the insane and the feral, with the princess the very worst of the bunch . . .

But he was so captivated by her beauty, he felt compelled to kiss her nonetheless. Instantly, she fell asleep, as did the rest of the castle's residents. And there they slept forever and a day without fear of awakenment.

Victims still of the old crone's double-edged curse . . .

*Paul Kane*

## THE PET LAMBS

Once upon a time, in an old farmhouse, lived a small girl, eight years old, called Little Bo-Peep; her father, Big Bill Taylor, raised cattle and sheep and her mother, Mary-Ann, looked after the house and the dairy.

Little Bo-Peep had two pet lambs, Sooty and Jet - Suffolk sheep have black faces - which had been brought up on a bottle, but were old enough now to join the flock in the meadow.

Big Bill was very, very worried because the wicked witch, Effandem, had been dropping evil germs on the sheep and cattle all over England and even into Essex, and the animals had to be killed as there was no cure.

Little Bo-Peep went down to the meadow to see Sooty and Jet; they came to her when she called. Suddenly there was a puff of smoke and there stood two little old ladies with bright, twinkly eyes.

'We are your fairy godmothers,' one said, 'and there is no need to be anxious about your lambs. Didn't you know that this is called Silly Suffolk? Silly from the old word Selig, which means 'Holy'. Wicked witch Effandem cannot fly over holy ground. Go and tell your father and mother.'

They vanished as quickly as they came and little Bo-Peep hurried back to the farmhouse with the good news.

*Elizabeth Brown*

## THE AMBUSH

Robin watched as Marion ran away into the den, crying pitifully, her dress stained. Something must be done. He had seen what had happened but hadn't been able to get there in time - now he'd make sure that nothing like that ever occurred again. Stealing from a defenceless girl was not to be looked upon lightly.

What could he do? A straightforward confrontation would be no use, because the enemy had so much strength on his side while Robin was yet quite small. There was only one thing for it: summoning his loyal friend John to his side, he outlined the plan. As they gathered the necessary equipment, it was nearing noon. Soon the sun would be high, and that would be too late.

Tying a last firm knot around the sturdy trunk of the oak, he surveyed the tripwire with satisfaction. John, across the woodchip path, nodded too. It was in just the right place. Scattering some leaves and twigs over the string to disguise it, Fatty Tuck joined his friends behind the dense green undergrowth. Robin smiled. Steve Nottingham had to pass through the playgroup garden on his way home for lunch because it was part of the school grounds.

Robin may have been only four, but no bully was going to steal his sister Marion's sweets and get away with it . . .

*S J Robinson*

# THE ODD COUPLE

Once upon a time there lived a man called Jack. Fit, streamlined body. Ate all the right things. No fat for Jack. He was so proud of his physique! His wife Jane was pretty. But pretty fat as well! Her passions were chocolates, fish and chips, and burgers.

Their son James had entered them in the school sports parents' race. You can guess which of the two was not looking forward to it!

The day came. Jack confidently toed the starting line, eager to begin, confident he would win.

Jane shook with fright, every inch of her a'wobble!

*Bang!* . . . off they went. Jack shot away from Jane. This was his hour!

Jane could only manage a trot with her bulk and soon became the back-marker! Then disaster struck! Jack's ankle cracked! He screamed with pain and pulled to a stumbling halt. All the other parents streamed past him. All except one! Up puffed Jane. All concern and worry.

'Oh sweetheart. Hold on to me my love and we'll reach the finishing line together.'

Slowly, ever so slowly, which suited them both! They did . . .

*Barbara Bradley*

## The New Cinderella

Once upon a time lived a big girl called Cinderella. She shared a large cottage with her two beautiful sisters, Mavis and Dolores, who were members of the famous pop group called the Nice Girls.

Our heroine was obese and her bloated face was covered with acne. Her ill-looks won her no friends. So, out of desperation, she had befriended a mangy flea-ridden mongrel dog she had acquired from the nearby animal sanctuary run by her fairy godmother. She called her new friend Prince, the namesake of the man of her dreams.

When Cinders walked past the animal shelter one day, she noticed a card displayed in the window which read: 'Big Gala Night, 22nd June - Kiss the Great Dane and behold he'll change into a Prince'.

The great day came, Mavis and Dolores wouldn't go to the 'do'.

'You don't know what you might catch slobbering over a dog,' they said.

Cinderella went to the fete alone. Throughout the evening all had tried for the star attraction and failed miserably except Cinders, who thought she'd give it a miss, until she heard her godmother urged her to try. The Dane gave a half-hearted growl, then fell silent allowing our heroine to plant a big kiss on the end of his nose. Suddenly he changed into a handsome prince.

It was love at first sight. Soon they were on their way to his mobile home in Mablethorpe, and they both lived happily ever after.

*David Ashley Reddish*

## THREE BEARS

Once upon a time there were three bears. There was Mummy Bear, Daddy Bear and Baby Bear and they lived in a cottage in the woods.

It was all right for Daddy, he went off to work every day. Mummy was content, making frilly things for the house. But Baby didn't stay a baby. He grew quite quickly on a diet of porridge, and was *bored*. Mummy told him stories about a naughty girl who broke people's furniture and spoiled their food.

'She ate their food,' Mummy Bear said, 'she nibbled it round the edges.'

'Naughty,' said Baby Bear.

Baby kept on growing bigger and more bored. One day he caught sight of himself in the mirror. There he was, quite a plump, well-grown bear dressed in *frills*. Mummy had made him a frilly shirt and wide-legged pants with frills round the bottom. The frills were bad enough, but she'd used leftover curtain material.

'There must be more to life than this,' Baby said to himself.

So, that night he ran away. He took his toothbrush and a clean shirt and just went. Mummy and Daddy were surprised when he didn't come for breakfast and asked each other where he could be, but then they forgot.

Baby Bear? He changed his name to Boy Bruin and joined a pop group. He wasn't a very good singer but the other boys weren't either. They wore frilly shirts made out of curtain material and called themselves 'Goldilocks'.

*Ann Harrison*

## THE PRINCESS AND THE PROPERTY MARKET

The princess was flicking impatiently through *The Guardian Angel Herald*, when a headline caught her attention - *'Jack in genetic modification scandal'*. She tutted to herself. What *had* he been thinking? He should have known it would attract attention, right outside his bedroom window for all to see! It had grown so fast, too!

She turned the page, and gasped. Centre page was an enlarged photograph of two beaming newly-weds. The caption read: *'Mr & Mrs Thumb, who were married Saturday last at, 11.30am, at All Sprites Church. Reception was held at the Bluebell Inn'*. The princess giggled in amazement. Thumbelina Thumb! Imagine!

Still giggling, she continued to cast a brief eye over the rest of the paper. Goldilocks, smilingly advertising *'Lorlikehell hair colour - Are you worth it?'* and *'Sleeping Beauty in Numbutotal drugs question!'* Now the princess was shocked - Beauty had always seemed so innocent! *'Wolfe cleared of Pigism and swine-ist remarks'*. She shook her head and 'Dear dear-ed' at the state of affairs in Fairyland.

When at last she found the property section, there was only one advertisement -

*'M Bellish & D Seeve, Estate Agents, are pleased to offer a desirable woodland residence. Off beaten track, rustic atmosphere, quaint furnishing. Private access to well and woodshed. Ideal for first-time buyers, hermits and/or socially unacceptable. Outside w/c, no chain. Viewing by appointment only'.*

'Not for me,' she thought, 'perhaps I should just take that pea from under my mattress?'

*S P Oldham*

## Are You Listening?

Throwing a saddle onto Moonbeam my cat, I laughed to myself, imagine believing those silly old stories, I was going to set out and prove everyone wrong. I hadn't gone very far before a pebble shot past my head blowing my best blossom crown to pieces,

'Be off with you,' a harsh voice shrieked, 'we don't want your kind round here.'

OK, I assured myself, this was just a one-off and the rest of my journey would be fine. We took a path deeper into the woods and settled down to lunch, I took the pips from my pack and as I was about to take a bite, an elf came from nowhere, snatched the rest of my pips and yelled

'That's what we think to outsiders, leave, go, out!'

Now I was beginning to think perhaps I had been a little bit silly and should have taken more notice of things I'd been told. We pressed on until we came to a pair of wolves.

'Lily, I smell trouble in these parts,' the first one growled.

'Me too, Lunar, there's only one way to deal with that, and it's to eat it all up,' howled the other.

Moonbeam ran home as fast as her paws would carry us, we ran in fear of our lives. So it was true, even after all these years, apple fairies were not welcome in the Forest of White.

*Nikky Ingram*

## CINDERELLA

Once upon a time, a lady called Cinderella lived with her stepmother
and two sisters.
One night, she switched on the 10pm news.
The Queen was planning a ball for Prince William's 21st birthday.
Cinderella gasped with delight, she was William's number one fan.
One ticket could be won to attend and have the first dance with the
Prince, if a viewer knew his favourite chocolate bar.
She grabbed her mobile phone and within five minutes, Cinderella had
won the prize.
'I shall go to the ball!' Cinderella cried.
She would have to be back by 12.15 am, (in time to make her
stepmother's hot chocolate).
She would wear her glass slippers, a gift from her late father, purchased
at the Princess of Wales' wardrobe auction.
Finally, Cinderella was at the ball and danced all night with the Prince.
Midnight arrived.
'I must go,' she whispered.
Cinderella dashed through the crowds leaving her glass slipper, he was
determined to find the owner.
The owner was traced to being Cinderella's father.
Meanwhile, Cinderella couldn't stop thinking about her amazing night
with the Prince and slipped into her glass shoe to relive the experience.
Just then, there was a loud knock at the door and she answered it.
There stood Prince William with her glass slipper in his hand.
'I think this belongs to you.'
'I think it does,' Cinderella sighed.

. . . and they both lived happily ever after.

*Samantha Drewry*

## JACK AND THE SUNFLOWER

Jack took the recently-born kitten into the village at the request of his mother. Times were hard and she thought the pet shop would offer payment that could help. As it happened, Jack was gullible and received payment by way of sunflower seeds and so received a clip around the ear from his mother on return.

'Rubbish,' his mother said, disgusted, and threw the seeds out onto the uncultivated plot of land at the back of the house.

In due course, a sunflower was seen growing at a tremendous rate five feet into the air until, at ten feet, it disappeared completely from view.

Meanwhile strange sounds could be heard in an adjacent garden and Jack peered over the wall to investigate *'Me I mow some - keep in trim and have some fun'* There he saw attractive neighbour Charlene singing whilst busily fitting a water feature, she was wearing a skimpy T-shirt and jeans. He was (though it has to be said would not admit) scared of her, after all she was a girl, Yuk!

In a few weeks' time Jack noticed the roots at the flower's base were pushing up the soil, on inspection he was amazed to discover a hoard of Roman coins. His mother was delighted and eventually, after a lot of legal wrangling, they received a large reward for the find.

Jack, it seems, was a natural at gardening and these days along with Charlene, hosts his own green-fingered show on television.

*Ann G Wallace*

## SPELLBOUND

It was a magical night. The full moon shone on every leaf, fern and toadstool. Glow-worms in the grass and fireflies in the air, added their lustre to the enchantment.

Two little girls, aroused from their slumbers, were surveying the scene from the window of a gypsy caravan. Their elders were still seated outside around a dying fire. A pile of snail shells, apple cores and husks of nuts remained of a supper gleaned from Nature's bounty. The dogs were eating the crumbs from rabbit pies. A whinny and a flick of a tail indicated piebald ponies at rest.

A light still shone from a window at the end of the village. The midwife had made her way to 6, Cobjoe Lane, a few hours before. A tired but happy mother now proudly held her first-born son in her arms.

In railway cottages, an elderly woman also clasped her long-lost son to her breast. Rejected by his childhood sweetheart Gilbert Greatorex had spent the last ten years in Australia. Kathleen, the love of his life, was now a widow. She had let it be known that another wedding ring would be welcome.

Two little girls, unaware of all this, looked as moonbeams fell on the fairy ring etched by fungus. Dressed in gossamer of rainbow hue, sprites and dryads danced round hand-in-hand to tinkling music. Hearing adult voices, the girls sought the comfort of bedclothes. Soon a pretence of sleep became the real thing.

*Vivienne Brocklehurst*

## THE SCRUBBER

Beth was a pretty teenager who lived with her dad John. He missed his wife, and she, her mother, but John was very lonely. He met a scheming woman with two very plain daughters. She was Gwen and she hated Beth, and made her do all the housework. She cruelly called her 'The Scrubber'.

The wife asked John for money, to buy dresses for herself and her two daughters to wear at the Mayor's Reception at the Town Hall. He said he was short of money.

'Sell your shares,' screamed Gwen, 'we can't go in rags.'

Beth of course wasn't included, so she went up to the attic to the old chest, which contained her dead mother's clothes. She had been dainty like Beth, and a white flower-sprigged dress was just the thing. Fancy little shoes as well, which just fitted!

The big night soon arrived, and the others went off in a hired cab. Beth put her things in a suitcase, and went by bus. She loved dancing, her mother had taught her, and very soon she met a tall young man, who whisked her on the dance floor.

He told her not to worry, he would see her home in his car. The others in her family hadn't noticed her in the big hall, and she arrived home before them. Glad rags soon came off, and she sat demurely in her chair.

The romance with Paul flourished, and they very soon got married. He was an accountant not a Prince, but he was 'her Prince', and she loved him!

*Edith Antrobus*

## THE LONG WALK

'Under, Sister-World, Brother-Moon, Father-Sky and on Mother-Earth
. . .'

Will remembered, as the otters jumped from the rocks and ran down
through the heather, some of these animals and beings, he had come
upon in those other realms - and those that had come upon him.
Especially the owls, they that had explained some truths of those realms
of strange and wondrous true colours.

Then there were Blackwings, Gold-tailed otters, of course, and Red
Foxes a'plenty! Robins and the Fireflies, Emerald Bees and the
Diamond-Fanged Timber Wolves, on the edge of 'Broken Oak' the
changed town.
Night Panthers and Whistler, in the haunted places.
Crimson Kingfishers. The Purple Phoenix.
The Five Geese of the lakes. Seagulls everywhere, and Ghost-Dragons
of dawn. A last Cave-Bear, and more, so many, many more . . .

Standing, Will closed his eyes and listened to his memory's voices, in
the morning mountain wind . . .

'See the Forest of Hopes.'
'Watch Whitetail.'
And that one whose voice spoke with most gentle sweetness, clearly
still.

'I'll wait by Rainbow Falls.'

And 'Running in Sunlight', there was no forgetting . . . a silver
memory.
Or, when the shadows fell across Tall Oak and everything changed, and
the good place became Broken Oak.

He remembered, too, the 'Crime' of truth, and the smell of smoke, and taste the ashes in the wind.

Burning timber, hopes and dreams - beauty swallowed in the all-consuming flames; and after in the quiet dark, a twinkling of embers and

*. . . magic!*

**Paul Holland**

## BABES IN THE WOOD

Once upon a time two little girls decided to go to play in the woods. Their mother agreed, but made them promise to be home for their dinner and to keep to the path.

This they did not do. Attracted by trees with hanging boughs of hazelnuts and bushes laden with brambles and wild raspberries they followed their noses, gorging themselves, and soon found themselves lost. Panicking, they tried to re-trace their steps, only to find that after a while they had returned to the spot where they originally discovered their mistake!

By now, it was obviously past their dinner time and night was beginning to fall. Luckily it had been a hot August day, so finding a patch of dry moss which was soft and warm they lay down on it and soon fell asleep.

Meanwhile, their mother had become worried and as soon as their father arrived home they organised a search party with some neighbours, a flashlight and a dog. Dividing into two groups, they searched the wood, calling and flashing the torch and the echo of the barking dog soon woke the girls. They and their parents were equally glad to be re-united, but on arriving home the girls wanted nothing to eat. They had had quite sufficient earlier and by the light of the kitchen tilley lamp looked a little green before being sick.

Ever after, they kept to the prescribed path in the woods lest they met with an accident or became lost again.

*Marjory Scott*

## THE LITTLE WOODEN BOY

The puppet boy Pinocchio broke free from his strings, swore, nicked Geppetto's cigs, stomped on the cricket that had been hanging around him getting on his nerves for months, and legged it into the night, free and happy at last, until he found himself alone in a dark forest with no stars visible for him to wish upon. Pinocchio felt lonely, tired, hungry and afraid.

Wolves howled in the darkness. A voice called out

'My Creatures of the Night. Vot musak they make. So awful. Shuuut Uppp!'

Something was thrown at a wolf. It yelped and the wolf pack went quiet for a moment then started howling again, as before.

Pinocchio suddenly saw a cloaked tall figure before him where only bats had flitted about moments before.

'Who are U, Child? Are you a runaway from home? Are you the puppet child Pinocchio everyone searches for? Why are you smoking at your age?'

Pinocchio denied all these accusations, which caused his nose to grow rapidly, just as the evil Count lunged forward, staking Dracula through the heart and turning him to dust, so Pinocchio returned home a hero and got a job assisting Buffy the Vampire Slayer.

*Arthur Chappell*

## THE THREE LITTLE PIGGIES . . .

Once upon a time there were three little piggies, who all lived together in a small wooden house in the wood.

One day, the Big Bad Wolf came wandering by, and knocked on their door.

'Little pigs, little pigs, let me come in.' But the little piggies squealed and cried:

'No, no, by the hair on our chinny chin chins.'

The Big Bad Wolf said: 'But I have some playing cards here, and I thought we could play Poker together.'

The three little piggies held a quick conference and decided that a game of Poker was just what they needed to brighten up the day (it was raining heavily outside).

So they let him in, and they all played Poker for two hours. The Big Bad Wolf had lost his shoes, his clock radio and his spare cash to the little piggies, and he was not in a good mood (being a Bad Wolf he seldom was, anyway).

The three little piggies tried to cheer him up by discussing their plans for new homes. Piggy number one was going to build his of straw, piggy number two was going to stay in the wooden one they currently shared, and piggy number three was going to build his new dwelling of bricks.

The Big Bad Wolf remembered his grandfather had had to huff and puff and blow houses down to get to his dinner, and decided 'What the hell?' and gobbled up his three little card-playing dinners there and then . . .

*Anne Rolfe-Brooker*

## THE FAMILY

I used to know a family of bears, Daddy, Mummy and baby Rupert. Times were hard, they lived in a tied cottage. Daddy lost his job so alas they became homeless. The good life, dreams for Rupert's future, all gone.

This was reality, they had to move on, hungry and cold, even with their thick coats on. They huddled together in the forest, not even a cardboard box to cushion the hard bracken on which they lay. Hunger drove them to look for food. They saw windows lit up and tables laden with fine food but when Mummy Bear knocked on doors, crying, 'Feed my child,' doors were slammed in her face.

The life of poverty got harder. Rupert was growing wild mixing with naughty bears who went about stealing porridge. The Bear family had discussed going abroad, now they would think seriously about this option. Mummy Bear sighed, 'Oh if this were a fairy tale we would all be transported to Yellow Stone Park, where all is peace and plenty and honey galore.'

She had no sooner spoken, when they were surrounded by sunshine which dappled the trees of the forest they now stood in. Small animals chattered a welcome to the Bear family who wept and smiled with joy.

So Mummy Bear got her wish, Daddy would not have to work so hard to feed his family and Rupert Bear was happy, he would travel the big forest and make new friends. They all got what they wished for. I do hope they lived happily ever after.

*Lily Izan*

## A Short Story Entitled 'A Sticky End'

I woke up with a start and jumped out of bed, for this was the day of reckoning! The hot spray from the shower stung as I planned my next move. I knew it wasn't going to be easy, but I had to find a way of defeating the old wizard, and only six hours to go before the deadline, when he threatened to turn everybody into jelly.

As I eased myself into my hyper-value suit and slipped on my plastic shoes, yes, you've guessed it, I come cheap. I had just finished drinking my second cup of Tesco coffee, when there was a thump at the door. I rose quickly with one hand on the handle and the other on my hot-water bottle. Damn, I forgot to pick up my gun! I've got to stop doing that. I flung the door wide open. There at my feet was 'The Beano'. Blast that paper boy, he never puts it through the letter box.

As I made my way downtown, on my Raleigh Chopper, I tried to roll myself a ciggy, but the rain didn't help. Oh well, I wanted to give them up anyway.

'Where have you been,' shouted Police Chief Cracker, that wasn't his proper name, but they reckon he was always on the pull!
'What do you intend to do about the old wizard?'
'Hey, that's my line.'
I told him quickly about my plan and his part in it. The idea was to entice the old wizard to the sweet factory, and while he was trying to make his mind up which to eat first, I could push him into the hot vat of liquorice and turn him into a Bertie Bassett.

The factory was deserted. The strong smell of sticky sweets nearly made me forget my task. I was just about to dip my finger into the candyfloss when I felt a sharp prod in my back. I knew my sweet tooth would get me into trouble one day. My legs quickly turned to jelly as I ran wibbly-wobbly. I caught a glimpse of myself in the window. Yikes, I am turning into a jellybaby. So the wizard had won again. So next time you open up a box of jellybabies, I will be the one holding the hot-water bottle.

*D J Smith*

## DOOR AJAR

The first Goldilocks never forgot her narrow escape from the Three
Bears. What is more, many of her small golden-haired descendants
woke up from nightmares of being chased through woods by bears,
until, at the close of the Twentieth Century, Little Goldi Lock decided
to discover if the Three Bears still lived in the woods.

She had a long walk because so much of the wood had been cut down to
make way for housing estates and parking spaces for a supermarket.
Seeing the latter gave her an idea. She might as well arrive prepared.

Outside the wood, she saw no sign that read 'Beware of Bears'. Perhaps
they had gone to live in a Safari Park? However, there *was* a sign which
read:
> *Private wood. Trespassers*
> *will be prosecuted*

Unafraid of being prosecuted - whatever that meant - Goldi set off
down a path that twisted among dark trees. Sometimes she heard
shuffling noises. Sometimes, eyes gleamed at her. She kept on going
until she reached a clearing.

Yes! A house with door ajar. Of course, in went Goldi and sat at the
table set for three. She ate the smallest porridge - but replaced it with
honey. Tired out, she slept on the smallest upstairs bed.

Delighted growls of 'Honey!' woke her up. As the Three Bears rushed
in, she held out her honey jar.

> *'For all three,'* she smiled.

Now a frequent visitor, the Three Bears call her Honeylocks. When she
grows up, she means to go into Advertising. Commercials for Honey
Products, perhaps.

*C M Creedon*

## HORNY

Once upon a time there was a Horny Flofinksus Parygowasky called
Horny! Well, actually it was an Ornithorhynchus Anatinus (or Duck-
Billed Platypus), but who on earth can get their tongue round *that* little
lot? So when my dad (who is a learned Professor) asked me to repeat
after him . . . it always came out as Horny Flofinksus Parygowasky
(well, I am only seven), so it's Horny for short!

Now, Horny was a right queer sort of mix-up! Well, what could you
expect from something that could only be found in the wilds of
Australia where everything is upside down, being on the underside of a
huge football called Earth, spinning its way through the sky!

Horny really was a great mixed-up kid. Neither fur nor feather, but a bit
of both. His mouth was a flattish beak like a duck's and he also had
webbed feet like a duck's too, but he also had a lovely slinky fur-
covered body that could slip through the water as easily as a fish!

Not only that, but his lovely wife didn't have babies like animals do. Oh
no! She laid eggs! Yes, real eggs that hatched out into lovely baby
Hornys that she suckled just as real animals do!

Mind you, not very many people have seen them, because they live
awfully secret lives and don't like anyone watching them. Some people
don't believe there are such things, but then some people don't believe
in fairies either (right stupid, they are). Just because they've never seen
one!

Me? Of course I believe in fairies! *And* I believe in Hornys too, even if I
have never seen one!

*G K (Bill) Baker*

## ALL HALLOWS EVE

All Hallows Eve is here again
The Devil's hand is on the rein
All things evil come out to play
So go home now and start to pray
Goblins, ghosts and evil ghouls
Looking for the souls of fools
Better make sure you have a sweet
When someone asks you 'Trick or Treat'
'Cause if you say 'Trick' it could cost
A devil's puzzle and your soul is lost
Don't trust anyone because as they say
If you sell your soul tonight you pay
Keep a watch out for witch and demon
They sometimes take the form of women
And watch out for werewolves and evil dogs
And stay away from toads and frogs
If my warning you do take
Then tomorrow morning you will wake
At home in your little bed
And forget all that I said.

*Paul O'Boyle*

## TOMMY THIN AND JOHNNY STOUT

Little Tommy Thin and Johnny Stout lived in the country and often played together. Neither of them had a tap at home. They had to be very careful with water even in very hot weather, they couldn't have a shower or turn a tap on for a nice cool drink because all water had to be carried from a well, over by the barn.

One fine day with the sun shining brightly, Johnny had to run an errand for his mother. Tom got rather bored, and wandered over by the barn. Later on, his errand finished, Johnny came sauntering along the road with a bag of chips. He loved chips and was always eating them, which helped to make him big and stout.

On the way there, he'd noticed two little girls playing by the barn with a kitten. Now coming back he saw that they were sitting by the well crying. He asked 'Whatever is the matter?'
They answered 'Our little pussy is down the well, and we can't get him out.'
'Who put him in?' Johnny said.
'That terrible boy Tommy Thin,' they replied.
He wanted us to play with him, and we didn't want to because he's not a very nice boy. He wanted our sweets, we wouldn't give them to him, so he grabbed our kitten and threw it down the well. We're frightened to look in case he's drowned.'

Then Johnny Stout went to the well and looked over the top. 'He'll be alright,' he said. 'It's just stuck on a ledge.' But the top of the well was narrow, and Johnny was big and stout, so as he reached down for the kitten he, too, got stuck, and the two girls had to hold onto him and pull, and pull until he was free. But the poor kitten was still down the well. Johnny then got a big stick, lowered the bucket down and gently pushed the kitten into the bucket and pulled it up. Out then jumped a wet bedraggled pussy, right into the arms of the little girls who, after thanking him, took it to their mother. She dried it with a towel and it sat by the warm radiator purring happily.

Their mother wanted to know what had happened. They told her that the poor kitten was in the well.

'So who put him in,' she asked, 'was it you?'

'No,' they replied, it was Tommy Thin.'
'What a naughty boy he was, to drown our poor kitty,' said their
mother, 'but who pulled him out?'
'Little Johnny Stout' they said. 'It was difficult but he managed it,' and
explained about him getting stuck.
'What a good boy he was,' she said, 'you must ask him here for tea
tomorrow.

When he got there, what do you think she cooked him for his tea? Egg
and chips, of course.

*Eunice Squire*

## JACK AND THE DODGY BEANSTALK

Once upon a time . . .

a lad rolled over in bed, bored with life, too lazy to get a job. He fancied the money, but not the idea of working.

Suddenly the bedroom door was flung open, his mother stormed in and pulled the duvet off, exposing his Simpsons boxer shorts. 'I'm fed up with keeping you. We've no money left and nothing to sell apart from one pig, so get your backside out of bed and go and sell it!'

Seeing the mood she was in, Jack thought he had better do as she said. He was blowed if he was going to walk, so he checked the tank on his bike for fuel and with a lot of squealing, shoved the pig into the sidecar. He was in a lot of strife when he got home again.

'You're a waste of space!' his mother screamed when he put a handful of beans on the table. 'They must have seen you coming.'

Jack couldn't believe his eyes the next morning. There was a dirty great beanstalk where Mother had flung the beans in disgust. He tried to see the top in the clouds and thought, 'I should climb up and snatch the goose that lays the golden eggs, but I can't be bothered.'

He could have saved himself a lot of grief, for as he turned his back, the giant started to come down, but because he had eaten too much, the beanstalk broke and he fell, squashing Jack.

*A Odger*

## PRIDE OF PLACE

Dino was a bright pink dinosaur. He lived in a beautiful bedroom where he had pride of place on the Satin bed. Red Devil was his mate, his black horns shining like a true devil's should. Scotty Dog and the Shaggy Twins all lived in the Satin bedroom, and they all wanted 'Pride of Place' on the bed. The mistress came in saying goodnight to all the furries. 'Be good till I get home,' she whined.

No sooner had she gone, the party started. The furries slid down the Satin bed singing and dancing while Red Devil breathed devils' fire. Then suddenly they heard the steps, 'Someone's coming.'

Everyone raced for their places, only in the turmoil they were in the wrong places. Mistress shook her head, Dino was not on the bed instead, Red Devil sat straight and tall. Glancing round she realised other furries were in different places. 'I'm just tired,' she mused and settled in-between the cool sheets and soon she was in Slumberland.

'Quick' shouted Dino, 'let's get to our normal place.' After much confusion, they returned to their normal places. Red Devil's disappointment showed and so did the others. Mistress awoke to find all normal.

'Must have dreamt it,' she thought, slipping back to sleep her dreams of 'Furries' Parties', or was it *'Fairies' Tricks'?*

*But Dino had his 'Pride of Place' and nothing more was said.*

*E Corr*

## TOBY

There once was a little dog, his name was Toby; when Toby wanted to go for a walk, he would say *'Woof! Woof!'* and he would fetch his lead, if it was raining he would put his front paws on the window sill and watch the rain, he would look back into the room with such a sad face, and give a tiny woof! and turn back to watch the rain splashing into the puddles.

Sometimes it was only a shower, or short rain, and he saw that it had stopped. He would scamper round the room with joy, giving little woofs of delight, Toby was a happy little dog.

When his excitement had quietened down a bit, he would 'Woof! Woof!' and collect his lead.

'Alright Toby, we can go out now, but you have got to behave, no running and rolling in puddles, I know you enjoy it, but when you shake yourself, you make me all wet, even if I have my wellie boots on and my yellow waterproof.'

Toby looked puzzled, he didn't know that it was naughty to do that, as he enjoyed it so much, but he wagged his tail as if he understood, oh joy his lead was slipped on, and he was in a hurry to be off.

Jack had on his yellow waterproof and his wellie boots, waved goodbye to Mummy, and Toby wagged his tail and gave a woof! Outside they both gave a happy whoop! and started to run, and before you knew it, Toby was into a puddle, and yes, he was having a roll in it, then he was out as Jack yanked on his lead,

Oh Toby! You naughty boy, Mummy will be cross, you have made me wet already, as Toby shook off all the water, Toby was astonished as at other times Jack hadn't minded at all, and in his joy at being out he was so happy he had forgotten that Jack had said, 'No rolling in puddles.' He looked at Jack with a woebegone expression which made Jack laugh, so Toby wagged his tail as if to say 'Sorry.'

So Jack said 'Oh well, let's run and we can get dry before we go back home to Mummy.' which they did, and they thought Mummy never knew.

*P Wright*

## HEDLEY

Once upon a time a man called Hedley searched for a smile. His search had taken him to faraway lands where he frequently became known as the stranger. After visiting hundreds of villages he at last came to a place where he sensed he belonged. The grass seemed greener here, the air was fresher. The first person he spoke to was pleasant and kind.

'I could settle here,' he said to himself.

He secured himself a job as a handyman at a local travel centre. Not many people went out but a lot of people came in. His new-found town was aptly called Settledown. He started dating a girl named Flo, she was a florist. They became inseparable and were soon Mr and Mrs.

Hedley looked in the mirror and discovered he had found his smile. He saw a lot of strangers passing through where he worked, he had a smile for each one of them. One person he noticed looked familiar, Hedley soon remembered who he was.

'Billy, what are you doing here?'

'What do you mean Hedley, you're the one who left.'

Hedley looked puzzled.
'But this isn't our village Reality!'

'Oh but it is, Reality had a boom time just after we discovered pleasantries, so many people wanted to live here, it grew into a town which we renamed Settledown town. The rate in which it's growing, we'll soon be renaming it Civil City.'

Hedley smiled ironically.

*John Beals*

## BEYOND THE STARRY PLOUGH

Beyond the starry plough rose an island from the sea and there lived a hideous wicked witch. Her evil magic bubbled and spat in a huge black cauldron.

She wore a long red ragged dress trimmed with blue and white lace. Upon her head perched a red pointed hat. Her fingernails were claws painted blue and white. She was a greedy witch with a magpie familiar.

She was in conflict with the inhabitants of a neighbouring island. It was so lush and green (a real gem of a place). She longed to possess it. But the people there had sought the help of a powerful wizard to stop her. The night sky was set alight with the frenzied battle of magic clashing and flaring. During the day the rivers turned to blood and the sun was blocked out by foul-smelling black smoke.

One day the wizard decided to try a different tactic. He took a mirror to the top of the highest mountain on the island and called upon the wind to blow the smoke away from the sun. The wind obliged, and as the witch aimed a particularly nasty spell at him, he turned the mirror towards her and caught it, reflecting it back on her. With a lot of fizzing and an almighty bang the witch disappeared in a huge cloud of green smoke. Destroyed by her own evil magic.

The wizard was a hero. The people were ecstatic and the island was safe again.

*Kim Montia*

## BANSHEE LANE

Begorrah! There were horrors in the Emerald Isle that night,
While the lightning flashed, and thunder crashed,
                         and rain lashed the town;
As the storm was raging overhead within the inky clouds,
Down below where the cobbled pathways wound,
In Banshee Lane there stood a dismal waxworks museum,
And inside that eerie dwelling awful terrors did abound.
Just before the midnight stroke tolled the old day out,
An uncanny wailing sound came sailing through the murk,
Enough to freeze your marrow, chill the blood inside your veins;
Through the grimy windowpanes I witnessed a waxwork
Start to stir, and from his pedestal proceed to slide;
And my heart began to labour like a tabor gone berserk.
While I was panicking, the mannequin came shuffling forth,
And the sight set my hairs a'ruffling on my scalp.
Armed with an axe, that man of wax was making tracks,
But much too terrified was I to think of crying for help;
For this was many moons ago, I beg you to remember,
And I was nothing but a young and highly-strung whelp.
The waxen executioner, dressed in sable cowl,
Made his weird way to where reclined a guillotine;
And all I had feared to be his foul design
Was proven to be true enough to make me turn quite green;
For then he knelt and placed his hooded head upon the block,
When the gore-encrusted blade swept down, I screamed like a colleen.
His noggin bounced across the floor and rolled to a halt,
And just as midnight tolled, he was bold enough to stare
Right into my horrified eyes that plainly saw
All the other waxworks turn my way to give a scare.
So away I hurtled like a hare without a backward glance,
Vowing nevermore to venture near that waxworks lair.

*Jonathan Goodwin*

## PEOPLE OF NIGHT

'It is late,
I sojourn too long
The wind is high
And I must journey
I bid 'goodnight' to my host
And open the door to
Step into the night alone

On the street
The Neon's pale glow
Throws shadows into
Dimly lit doorways
A mist rises, and, in the mist
Something stirs
A shaft of light falls
Onto a pale, tall, gaunt,
Hound-like figure
Its stark eyes glare
As it draws a grimace
Over blackened yellow teeth

I lengthen my gate
As the spectre flits
From shadow to shadow
I hurry along
And, glancing over my shoulder
As on the wind I witness
The spectre's call

The spectre leaves the
Shadows to tag me
And as I turn and run
Glides hollow behind, then
Above, its claws like hands
Tear at my hair
And flying scarf

Bent low running
I reach the open road
'I cross' and bang the door
Furiously I fumble
With my keys
I open the door and enter
Slamming the draw bolt tight

Dishevelled I fall
Exhausted in the hall
And as I fall I glance up
At the pale claw like hand
At the open parlour window

Empty street bare
Whom lurk there
In gloomy shadow
Beneath neon glare

People of night
In darkness hide
Their muffled feet
O'er cobbles glide

Shadows of night
Mask their scowl
But hush wind
Hark they wail

An echo sharp
Two beats apart
Strikes cold fear
Deep to heart

Fleet nimble feet
Tip tap beat
Echoes hang listless
O'er barren street

Hurry feet fleetly
Guide me home
Never again dare
Walk night alone.

Em'm nobody about
Still early yet
Pubs haven't closed
Still quiet for a
Saturday night
Cold, must fix my tights
There, now fix my make-up
Neon's dim tonight

A dog's awailing
Ought to be in on
A night like this
Shameful, its master
Ought be prosecuted

Oh, there's a gentleman
Now, must make a few bob
I'll just step forward
'Hello Dear' But wait,
What's that in the shadows
'Oh my Gawd' It's no gentleman'
God have pity I'm off
'Feet don't fail me.'

*R J Collins*

## THE SPIRIT BRIDE

When, a few years ago, we were house-hunting, the opportunity came for us to buy an old disused church and its grounds. We jumped at the chance. For one thing, the price was much better than those of the other properties we had considered. The other point in its favour was that the delightful old building invited us to make a pleasant, unusual home.

The old vestry was just the right size for conversion to a kitchen which, having saved money on the purchase, we could afford to have fully fitted. My carpentry-trained husband's eyes shone as he saw the wood of the pews and the choir stalls, and these were soon used to make a dining suite and a desk. We kept the stained-glass windows, (which made brilliant, kaleidoscopic patterns when the sun shone), made a luxurious floral display for the old font and placed the television on the vantage point of the pulpit. We carpeted the stone floors and left the ornate altar in place to hold plates and ornaments. There was, unusually, an upper floor where the Sunday school once met, so we were able to furnish bedrooms and have a bathroom fitted.

Whilst we were busy with the conversions we went to bed each night exhausted and slept soundly through the hours of darkness. Later, however, once we were able to relax during the day, we began to hear noises at night, such as organ music (though we had discarded the ancient organ) and the sound of sobbing and footsteps outside the bedroom door. Our son, a cynical sixteen year old, explained, with elaborately obvious patience, that the noises were caused by nothing more sinister than the trees outside and the old walls and flooring of our new home.

In the spring we held a house-warming party. As the guests toured our new home we basked in their praise and appreciative remarks as our conversions were examined. The celebrations lasted till the small hours of the morning and, uncharacteristically, our son, David, set up a deckchair in the front garden after lunch and went to sleep in the warm spring sunshine. As I approached my front door after gathering some daffodils for the dinner table I saw a girl - young and very pretty - in a white dress, her hair adorned with white flowers and pearls.

She smiled and indicated I should go inside. Bemused, I obeyed, and found that the interior of my house looked very different. Once again it seemed to be a church, lit by candles, the pews filled with people, beautifully dressed, listening to a cheerful organ recital, and I sensed an air of excited expectancy.

I sat down on the back pew and then David, looking rather like a zombie, walked down the aisle to the front. The people on his side of the church turned and smiled at him as he made his entrance. There was the scent of spring flowers and I saw that the place was beautifully decorated, floral arrangements everywhere - most of the flowers wild, but attractive.

Now the girl I had seen earlier entered, linking the arm of an elderly man, smiling contentedly. She was followed down the aisle by four little girls who looked as if they might be her sisters. They, too, were dressed in dazzling white, ribbons in their hair and they carried baskets of wild flowers. The party reached the front of the church and marriage vows seemed to be being exchanged. I couldn't be sure just what was happening, however, because I had suddenly begun to feel a sort of faintness and the scene became fuzzy, so I was forced to close my eyes. When I opened them I found myself sitting on one of the benches we had placed around the wall of the main room of our home.

I went out into the sunshine and my son was still sleeping in his deckchair. When he woke up he said nothing, except that he had had 'the strangest dream' - but he enlightened us no further. Later that year he left school and started a college course in London, and life continued quietly in our old church-home.

It must have been a few months later when I went to a jumble sale in the local village hall. Among the goods for sale I noticed an old portrait and gasped: 'That young man looks exactly like David - my son!' I said to the volunteer seller behind the table. 'Does he, indeed?' she asked. 'He was a lovely young man, I believe, but the whole thing was so tragic.' I asked her what she meant and she told me a story she said she was surprised I hadn't already heard. I hadn't:

During the nineteenth century a beautiful young servant girl came to work in the vicarage and fell in love with the vicar's handsome young son. Her feelings were reciprocated and, after some initial difficulties because of their social differences, the young couple, given permission to become engaged, began to plan their wedding the next spring. Everything seemed to be going well and the day of the planned wedding was bright and sunny, daffodils waving in the churchyard in the Easter breezes. All the guests were assembled. The bride and her attendants arrived but the bridegroom did not . . .

. . . After a very tense waiting time the guests departed, embarrassed. Of course, the general gossip was that the girl had been jilted at the altar, and many cruel jibes were made about servants trying to climb higher than their allotted status. The girl, however, refused to believe that her lover could possibly have been so cruel.

That evening the news came that the bridegroom had had an accident as he made the short journey from the vicarage to church. Suddenly startled, the horse leading his carriage had bolted, throwing him into a ditch at the side of the road. This need not have been fatal but the young man landed awkwardly and broke his neck.

His tragic bride refused to leave the church, certain he would come to claim her. There she stayed, resisting all entreaties for her to come away, until one day she was found dead, starved of food and worn down by her emotion. She was buried in the little churchyard beside the vicar's son.

There were, I remember, 'goose pimples' on my arms as I left that jumble sale carrying a portrait I had just purchased. Rubbish, though! I don't believe this kind of thing any more than you do! All the same, after that peculiar experience of mine - ours - the strange noises at night stopped. Also, in the little graveyard at the back of our church-house there was, indeed, an old gravestone, engraved: 'Here lie the mortal remains of David Jerome Colworthy, beloved son of the Rev Jacob Colworthy, Vicar of this church, and of his wife, Ada. Also Mary Jemima Peterson, the cherished betrothed of the above David Jerome Colworthy. May they rest peacefully together after their tragic and untimely deaths.'

*Rosemary Yvonne Vandeldt*

## MOMENT OF TRUTH

My heart started beating loudly in my chest
and I could hardly contain myself.
I had been waiting all my life for this moment
and I knew when it eventually came, I would know immediately.
As I glanced at this perfect being beside me - I knew I was in love.

*Janet Jeffrey*

## MAN OVERBOARD!

Waves crashed over the side of the ship, a voice was heard,
'Man overboard! to the rear of the starboard bow.'
The small life raft was thrown to the waiting man.
Then another voice was heard.
'The water will be getting cold Stephen,
It's time you got out of the bath.'

*Mandy Ann Cole*

## A Change Of Plan

Before serious chest pains had given him cause to visit his doctor
the budding author's plan had been to have many books
of his own material published.
Now his plan was to enjoy every moment left.

For his life wasn't going to be as long as he thought it was.

*Danny Coleman*

# THE LITTLE GHOST WHO COULDN'T GO BOO

There once was a little ghost,
Who couldn't go boo,
He couldn't frighten me,
He couldn't frighten you,
When he came out at night,
No one got a fright,
He couldn't even frighten mice,
He simply was too nice,
He tried groaning,
He tried moaning
He went to great pains,
A-rattling his chains,
But he still wouldn't frighten you out of your brains,
Then a nice couple moved into his street,
They wanted a friendly ghost to make their home complete,
Now he's the answer to all of their prayers,
As you hear his footsteps come down the stairs,
Now they leave him his supper at bedtime,
When at midnight the clock does chime,
He gives them an early morning call,
By giving a groan in the hall,
So they live a blissful life,
The ghost, Mr Jones and his wife.

*Alan Pow*

## WHITE ROSES

Do you believe in ghosts? I don't. Or at least, I didn't. Now I'm not so sure. Surely they are an invention of those who are afraid to accept their own mortality? The possibility that when we die we are no more, dust to dust, ashes to ashes. Or of unscrupulous money grabbing charlatans, intent on persuading the bereaved that their loved ones live on in another dimension and can be contacted through the chosen few who have supernatural powers. Of course, there are those who only half-believe and enjoy the sensation of fear through eerie tales of chain rattling spectres and headless wraiths. Craving revenge for past wrongs. Each and everyone, self-deluding. Or are they?

Perhaps it's best to keep an open mind, to tread a path between naive credulity and outright cynicism. Let me tell my tale, and perhaps you will agree.

The biting north wind tore through my warm coat and howled through the majestic trees that formed the boundary to the grounds of the old house, that was an annexe to the local hospital. No one knew how many occupants had lived there between the turn of the century and the time in the 1950s when it passed into the hands of the local health authority. Mass screening for tuberculosis and new drugs to treat it had created a need for a sanatorium. The newly diagnosed who were in the early stages of the disease were housed in one storey prefabricated buildings dotted around the grounds but those with more intractable chest problems were accommodated in the house, and we usually had between twenty and thirty patients at any one time in this area. The wide entrance hall was warm and welcoming. Double glazing and central heating had eliminated the draughty corridors and ice patterned windows of earlier times, and electric lights illuminated the darkest corners. It was my second month of night duty, and I had adjusted to sleeping in the daytime and felt refreshed and rested, ready for whatever the night might bring.

Legend had it that the house was haunted by the restless spirit of its earlier owner, who at the turn of the century was abandoned by the man she loved on the eve of her wedding day. She was said to have hanged herself from the dark wooden balcony with a silk scarf. The more fanciful said she was doomed for eternity to retrace her footsteps up the staircase and along the balcony because her sad spirit could find no peace.

No one I knew had ever seen the 'grey lady', had not seen a glimpse of a ghostly ankle there or anywhere else for that matter. But the legend persisted. My fellow nurses and I would have given a month's wages to catch sight of her and many a midnight hour found at least two of us sitting on the stairs willing 'our' ghost to appear. Not that we were brave, we were not, but having a companion gave us courage. It became a game we played on quiet nights to while away the time until dawn broke. Despite its eerie reputation, I loved the old house, It was gracious, warm and cheerful and it seemed to me that whatever dreadful event took place there, no bad vibrations lingered to trouble the living.

Summertime would find me taking my breaktime in the lovely gardens. The well-kept lawns and colourful flower beds gave it an air of tranquillity that complemented the weathered ivy-covered wall of the house. My favourite spot was the bench next to the rose garden, where I ate my sandwiches and listened to the birds singing and the bees in the lavender hedge. The rectangular rose garden was full of white scented roses, from snowiest white to palest cream but all with the sweetest smell. It was said that the 'grey lady' planted this bed in honour of her forthcoming virginal bridal bed, and the white rose tradition was maintained. As rose bushes died they were replaced with newer, hardier species but always with white scented bushes.

If I close my eyes I can still conjure up that intoxicating perfume of those roses of forty years ago. Those of us who were fascinated by the tale would speculate on the physical form of the spectre. She would be young and very beautiful, we all agreed her pale grey diaphanous gown would float softly around her as she glided as soundless as a butterfly's wings up the stairs and along the landing. We would stare in morbid curiosity and wonder at just what place those elegant legs had dangled.

As time went by, I forgot all about ghost hunting. Nothing was further from my thoughts as I climbed the stairs on that chilly night, glad to be out of the wind and cold. Several patients were on the first floor landing and I greeted them all by name.

A middle-aged woman with a steel grey plait hanging over one shoulder came out of the office and went through the door of the second single room on the left. Her grey woollen dressing gown swept the floor and was loosely tied around her matronly figure. She appeared not to notice me, so preoccupied with her own thoughts was she. The room had been vacated two nights ago when the elderly male patient was transferred to the general hospital, suffering from acute pneumonia.

Checking the register for new admissions, I could find no record of one, so puzzled but not at all alarmed I went to the door and knocked softly. When there was no response I opened it and went in. The room was as it was left two night ago. The bed was freshly made and the locker bare of personal items that indicated recent occupation. Every room was checked but everyone was where they should be and every vacant room empty. I asked several of the patients if they had noticed a new one and none had. 'You're pulling our legs' was the response from my co-workers when I told them of my disappearing patient, and I too began to suspect a practical joke at my expense but they all denied any knowledge of it.

Later I did a routine check of the ward, still not convinced that I had not been a victim of some bizarre prank, but all the patients were peacefully sleeping and all was quiet and still.

Something prompted me to open the second door on the left just once more. I giggled softly as the crazy thought crossed my mind that she was probably hiding under the bed or in the wall closet.

On the window ledge above the radiator stood a bowl of white roses. Their distinctive fragrance wafted across the room as the goose-bumps rose on my arms.

*Mair Patchett*

## NOT ALONE

Very stealthily and with bated breath I tip-toed up the stairs to investigate an uncanny intermittent creaking under the floorboards as I knew I was alone in the house.

Very gingerly I crept across the first landing to hide in an alcove of one of the many passages of this great Victorian house, thinking to myself 'What a lot of work the poor servant girls had to do.' These houses with a drawing room , dining and sitting room, conservatory, nursery suite, lounge, kitchen, pantry, scullery, larder, cellar, morning room, library, study and laundry room. Not forgetting the huge gardens. When suddenly there was a great 'Bang', followed by complete darkness. Next a light so bright, as if the sun had dropped from the sky and all hell let loose! I froze paralysed by shock and fear so tense, I could hear the sound of my heart beat, blood flow and temperature drop to near zero as I shivered uncontrollably. Then I awoke.

*Gill Ives*

## THE PRINCESS AND THE GOBLIN MARKET
*(A pre-Raphaelite Fantasy)*

'She has gone to the Goblin market, where unwholesome fruit is sold', thus spake the aged figure. Once a serf, then a lover to his lady, now lonely in his tower.

He strode about the rooms, avoiding those places where he knew the floorboards were rotten. Fruits were piled in corners, bruises browning the russets and greens. Mice peeped through holes in tapestries.

In the room of her Great Great Grandmother he found only rose petals, dry, withered. He gathered them in his callused hands and buried his face in the fragrant mass.

'She had gone to the goblin market, where unwholesome fruit is sold', whispered the vassal. The sun now hung low above the lake of eventide. Autumn's own colours draped across the sky.

In his heart he saw her undo the tresses, the grey burning away as the welkin's gold and crimson flowed amongst her own once-titian locks. The scarlet of her dress, the Carnelian's on her finger and at her ears. The sanguine lady who now trod a damned pathway.

'She had gone to the goblin market, where unwholesome fruit is sold', thus the tale was repeated in the kirk by the cleric, at the watermill by the farmer, in the encampment by the gypsy-fiddler, in the woods by the charcoal burner, in the field by the shepherd, in the street by the beggar.

And Sir Curdie threw the rose petals on the fire.

And the smoke brought a tear to his eyes.

*Cardinal Cox*

## DING, DONG THE BELLS WILL CHIME

Cinderella didn't meet her Prince Charming at a dance, she met him at her friend's wedding. The ugly sisters didn't want her to go but she climbed out the bedroom window and took a taxi to the church. As she was coming out the church, David touched her on the shoulder and said, 'I like your hat and hair.' Cinderella giggled and said,' Would you like to borrow them.' David followed her to the gate and looked at her shoes. 'I like your shoes,' he said smiling then looked at the bride and groom. 'You would look lovely in a wedding dress.' Cinderella, took off her shoe and gave it to David. 'I think I have a little stone in my shoe.' David examined the shoe and smiled. 'Ah, yes, I think this shoe belongs to you, can you try it on?' Cinderella sat on the seat and tried the shoe on. 'It's amazing how the shoe is a perfect fit. Does that mean we can get married next week and have our honeymoon in Paris.' David said, 'Once my divorce comes through, there could be a possibility, I think.' Cinderella held out her hands and David pulled her up. She said, 'Can I give you a lift to the wedding reception?' David nodded. In the car, Cinderella said, at the traffic lights, 'My two ugly sisters will be very jealous, when I tell them the news.'

*Kenneth Mood*

## JACK'S TALL TALE

'Right Jack. One more time. Where did you get this property?' ie one 'golden-egg' laying chicken, one 'golden talking harp'; and one large quantity of golden coinage with a street value of thirty thousand pounds.' 'I've told you before. Now just leave me alone, will you.' 'Can't do that son. Got to get the story clear. It's very important. You may need to rely on it later.' 'All right. I'll tell you again.'

'Me and Mamma were very poor right. So she ordered me to sell our only possession, Daisy our cow. Anyway, always needing money for 'essentials like' I went out to see what I could get for her. Then I bumps into a dealer friend of mine who offered me some magical beans. I knew this dealer well and he hadn't let me down before so I trusted him. How was I to know what would 'appen. Anyway, not coming back with the dosh led to an almighty row and Mamma chucked the beans out the window.

Before I knew it, this enormous green thing grew up into the sky. So trying to escape Mamma's rage I climbs up. And it's when I'm there that I meet this really tall geezer. He tried to blinking kill me. So I nicked all his stuff and legged it. He follows, trips and breaks his neck.'

'Ha! A right tall tale. Jack, as an officer of the law I am arresting you on robbery, manslaughter and the misuse of drugs.

*Michael Bellerby*

## LUCY GETS HER MAN

Lucy was the youngest in a dysfunctional family. Often she was verbally abused by her step-sisters, while her father neglected her as her step-mother thought she was her personal slave. Lucy was happy when left to her own devices. Her only friend was the local pizza delivery boy, with whom she discussed her plans for escape.

Lucy had heard there was to be a street party, the major and his son were going. No one had asked Lucy to attend but her step-sisters were going to view the available talent.

On the appointed day of the do, with no thoughts of it in mind Lucy entered a charity shop. In the shop was an old friend of her mother's. She too was browsing, she picked up a dress for Lucy to try on. The old lady said it fitted Lucy like a glove. With a cheap hairslide, dabof make-up - transformation complete. 'Come to the party with me,' she said, 'You look splendid.'

The major's son felt his heart stop as Lucy alighted from the old Mercedes. None of Lucy's family recognised her and after one dance the major's son was smitten. But Lucy had a time limit, rushing back to the old woman a shoe fell off, (delicate gold strappy number).

A notice appeared in the paper asking the owner to reclaim her property. Pizza boy said to Lucy, 'Hop on my bike, I'll take you to claim your prize - the major's son and a way out of slavery.'

*S Mullinger*

# THE TALE OF THE GLORIOUS BISCUIT

Once upon a time there lived a biscuit in a box. It watched all the other biscuits disappearing one by one, until it was the last one left. Fearful of being similarly consumed, it formulated a plan in its biscuit brain, and sat back to see how things developed.

One day a little girl opened the box, and was about to reach in to snatch the biscuit out, when it spoke.
'You can't eat me! I have been transformed into a thing of glory,' it said.
The little girl paused, and looked down sceptically.
'You don't look very glorious to me,' she said,
'That's only on the outside,' the biscuit replied. 'Inside, I shine with the brightness of the stars, and am made of the stuff of legends.'
'Oh well, I'd better leave you alone then,' she said, and skipped away.

The very next day a little boy opened up the box, and was about to reach down and gobble the biscuit up, when it spoke.
'You can't eat me! I have been transformed into a thing of glory,' it said.
The boy didn't reply, but his eyes opened a little wider, as if in awe.
'Before space was formed, or even there were an earth and a sea, I shone,' said the biscuit.
The boy paused, drawing near to the biscuit as if to verify its claims, only to grab it and munch it down.
'I never ate a thing of glory before,' the boy said, smiling.

*Allen Baird*

## THE SPIT AND POLISH BOYS

As everyone's eyes fixed upon a pair of black boots, shining in the midday sun, spurs reflecting the sunrays and the sound of little bells on the end of his spurs. People started to run crying out. The Spit and Polish boys are in town.

Slowly you could see more of the boots until a tall figure in shiny black leathers from head to toe. It's one of Dragstar Kings from the spit and polish boys.

People run in to the safety of their homes as he marched into the corner bar, and with his strong voice, 'Coffee black' in a demanding manner, 'Yes Sir!' the man behind the counter said, his hands shaking.

'Please don't drink it too fast as my coffee machine will not make coffee as quickly as you drink it,' trembling as he said that.

'Fill it up' the boots said, 'yes sir But! But! slow down please.' After seventeen cups the spit and polish boys staggered out of the bar!

People peeping from behind their doors, he mounted his Yamaha Dragstar 1100cc and with a press of a button, he rode off out of town, to the relief of the townspeople.

Must they live in fear for the next day they will appear? They were remembering last year, when thirty of the spit and polish boys came to town. They drove the town crazy and drunk the town right out of coffee. They gate crashed in the townfolks' homes and places of work and ordered them to make coffee and paid them with petty cash. There was not a drop of coffee to be had for weeks after they had left. It was only twelve weeks later when it was another sad day for Makeoverville.

That day, it was Friday the 13th, everyone was going about their shopping, when they heard in the distance the throbbing of engines, like in the last war when the planes came over. Then someone cried out, 'It's the spit and polish boys.'
Everyone ran, a woman grabbed her children and ran into their homes.

The shopkeepers started to board up their windows and then the sound of the spit and polish boys as they all lined up at the old Corral. Their boots shining in the sunlight and their black leathers shining bright blinding all the passers by. Then they entered the corner bar. 'Coffee for us all,' they said.

'Yes, yes!' shaking with fear, said the barman.

They went crazy that day. Old Mrs Mackintosh, she was in a bath filled with coffee and a gang of the spit and polish boys armed with straws, sucking away like mad. You could hear her cries for miles. Many of the bikers gate-crashed in on Farmer Johns, they had his wife making coffee non stop, and all at the same time, poor Mrs Johns! Then they dragged old Mr Woods into the bar, sat him down at the piano and said 'Play!, play Tea For Two.'

Only the spit and polish boys were singing Coffee for Two, three, four, five and six all of good upstanding sound, you understand. All the birds suffered, the two legged ones I mean. When all of a sudden in came the local Bobby, you could hear a pin drop, the few villagers that were in the bar moved to the side, except for the party girls. They were too full of coffee to move away. When one of the Spit and Polish boys, turned as if to go for his wallet, he paused and said 'Coffees all round.'

Had the local Bobby lost his mind when he said 'You all will be quiet when you leave town.'

Was there going to be a showdown? Was there going to be a drink-out at the old Corral? What a relief when the Spit and Polish boys left town that day. As they mounted their Dragstar 1100cc and rode out of town, but not before taking their yellow dusters out of their pockets and polishing the dust off their bikes.

Old Mrs Mackintosh, she is coffee coloured all over her body now, and it will be a long time before Mrs Johns will be making coffee for her husband again. As for the local Bobby, has he lost his senses wanting coffee when the Spit and Polish Boys are in town? When will they next come to town? And how many will they be next time? Will they drink the town dry? Will the town folk survive another day?

Keep a look out for the next episode on the Spit and Polish boys . . .

*Paul Volante*

## PRINCE EVAN AND THE GIANT BEES

Princess Aimee was paralysed, an insect had stung her on holidays in Greece. King Nathan sent for all the specialists in the world but they could not cure her. Prince Evan dreamt that the princess had been bitten by a rare mosquito. The only cure was honey from the giant bees thousands of miles away in the dark jungle. Prince Evan told the king about his dream.
'If you cure her we will give you her hand in marriage.'
Prince Evan had always loved the beautiful princess.
He went to see his Friend Ashley who had a helicopter.
'I will fly you there but I am too afraid to go into the jungle' he said.
Ashley flew him there, dropped him off and waited.

Prince Evan could hear loud buzzing and the flapping of wings. He went near the large honeycomb but he did not know how to get inside.
'What are you doing you silly man?' asked a very large butterfly. Evan told her about the princess.
'I will help you but you must hide under the toadstool or the bees will kill you, I won't be long.'
The butterfly came back with honey in a large cobweb.
'Hurry the bees are coming,' she said and flew him quickly back to Ashley.

Prince Evan was the first person to ever come out of the jungle alive. Princess Aimee ate the honey and was cured. The King kept his promise and Princess Aimee and Prince Evan lived happily ever after.

*D A Fieldhouse*

## PRINCESS AND THE FROG

Once upon a time, a beautiful but extremely vain and selfish girl named Princess, sat admiring herself by her large garden pond. Suddenly, a football splashed into the water, soaking her in the most disagreeable manner! (It had been kicked with gusto by the Loverpull hopeful next-door.) Furious, Princess decided to confiscate the ball and with arms outstretched, vainly tried to reach it. Her only solution would be to go in after it - an abhorrent idea, as it would undoubtedly ruin the extremely expensive Savucchi dress she was wearing! A frog eyed her dilemma from a nearby lily pad. Angrily, she grabbed for him but he managed to escape and she found herself crushing his now vacant lily pad, in her hands.

'Princess,' he croaked, from his new spot on the offending ball, 'I will bring this ball to you if you promise to let me sleep on your pillow tonight, for you have surely crushed my bed.'

Slyly, Princess agreed, having no intention of keeping her promise. Immediately, the frog dutifully brought the ball towards her.

'Never will you sleep on my pillow!' cried Princess, lurching for the ball in front of her. Suddenly, she slipped, promptly falling into the pond, where the frog planted a slimy kiss right on her cheek! All at once, Princess changed into the largest, most beautiful lily pad imaginable! Grinning wickedly, the frog hopped onto the lily pad, happier than ever-after all, this was so much better than sleeping on an old pillow, any day!

*Lucy Loretta Hegarty*

## SNOWIE WHITE AND THE SEVEN DWARFOES

Snowie White was conceited. She did not like being with friends prettier than herself, so she picked her friends with care. The Seven Dwarfoes were ideal, all undersized, all adoring her.

Her father's partner was jealous of her, and decided to teach her a lesson, and disguised herself as a poor woman selling apples.

'Would the pretty lady like an apple?' she wheedled.
'No, don't, Snowie,' Fatso tried pulling her away, but Snowie didn't like being told what to do, and pushed him away.
'This nice red one, to match your rosy cheeks' the old hag held one out, temptingly.
Snowie took it eagerly, bit into it, and staggered backwards, the apple stuck firmly in her throat. With a little sigh, she sank down, unconscious.

The Seven Dwarfoes pushed and pulled until they had her on a makeshift bed, and then sat wondering what to do next.

It was then that a young man passed by, riding a clapped-out bicycle. He was no Prince Charming - in fact he was very ugly. He looked at the unconscious Snowie, and fell in love with her.

Clumsily stumbling against the support of her makeshift bed, he caused it to collapse. Snowie went crashing to the floor, jolting the apple from out of her throat. Opening her eyes, she saw the ugly young man - knew he was the man for her, as he would not compete with her for looks. So, she stretched out her hand to him. 'My Prince!' she murmured.

*Joyce Hockley*

## ALICE'S NIGHTMARE

'Off with her head,' said one,
'Leave her for dead,'- she's done!
- drowning deep amongst the frauds,
who seemed to be on all the boards!
                    - Poor Alice!

'I did so want to be free -
free - just to be me, me, me -
but for every freedom they promise, you see,
There's always a very substantial fee!'
                    - sighed Alice!

As Alice grew smaller and smaller,
eating the GM bread supposed to be making her taller -
she then suddenly awoke,
and found it was all only a joke!

No - it had all been a nasty dream -
no fat cats out there, licking up all the cream,
or trying to trick others with every scheme,'
                    - exclaimed Alice.

Now - it was to be a world of love and peace,
where all wars and crimes would forever cease;
                    - 'Thank God' said Alice.

'No more a cold, hard, greedy world;
with nations' flags all being unfurled!'
                    - declared Alice.

'A new kingdom here on Earth;
a promise now of our rebirth
- not the Book of Revelation,
but the promise of triumphant jubilation,
                    - no more malice!'
                    exhorted our Alice.

*Bea Wilson*

# ELSA POPPIN

The race meeting was starting tomorrow,
It would be a social delight,
After the races had finished
Disco dancing would end the night.
Elsa from the house on the corner
Was begging to be able to go,
But stepmother was turning quite nasty,
And the answer was always *'No!'*
'Of course your sisters are going,
The King of the bikers will be there.
He's looking for someone to marry,
And I'm sure he'll choose one of my pair.'
The eve of the dance had duly arrived,
Elsa was tearful and sad,
A knock on the door was insistent,
When she opened it My! was she glad.
For there on the step was a parcel,
Of leathers, the brightest blue.
They fitted dear Elsa quite snugly,
And she knew she looked beautiful too.
She went to the dance that evening,
It was a romantic affair.
All night the King was her partner,
Because nobody else would dare.
At last the evening was over.
The King and the girl said farewell.
He said he would phone her next morning.
He had something to ask her as well.
Stepmother was simply furious,
Her girls couldn't possibly win.
For the King had fallen for Elsa
And asked her to marry him.

The wedding was in the springtime,
And in true Fairy Tale style.
They both lived 'happy ever after',
At least for a little while.

*E Timmins*

# FLINT ARROWHEAD

I am Pip - from Fletchers row - I've lost my way
I am Simon - you're not from round here
Come on I'll help you find your way
Pip came into this world - a century and a half ago
Bare feet dressed in rags - was small for his age
They searched high and low - the answer was no
I am lost - I can't get back - Pip began to cry
There's no way back - no way - I am truly lost
We can always hope - always try - came Simon's reply
We'll keep looking - there's a way back - don't fear
Many a moon had passed - since people lived round here
They've moved away - to pastures new
They'd searched all day - this is all they knew
I've an idea - find a glass - I've a candle
I know Mum would say no
Always hope - always try - we'll give it a go
As the flame began to dance - they watched it dance
Follow the light Pip - follow the light - was the chant
I am scared Simon - I am scared - was Pip's reply
Follow the light - always hope - always try
Soon Pip's shaky voice - turned to echo - and was no more
Safe journey - friend - safe journey
Soon day turned into night - I hope he'll be OK
On an open window sill - a flint arrowhead - caught
The light as night turned into day - and all was OK.

*David Charles*

## WATCH THIS SPACE

Mine's an old house inhabited by woodworm.
I shouldn't have used that boiling tar.
Now it's war!
There's a ring of holes appearing round my armchair.
Thousands of tiny heads!
They've obviously eaten the plasterboard ceilings
In line . . .
Seems I'm off to the basement any moment.
Watch this space.

*James Kimber*

# PIT STOP OR NOT?

Tension mounts in the pit lane.
It's a crucial stop.
Tyre pressure checked, and the fuel nozzle's connected.
Time's running out, will he make it on time?
He's not going to make it, one car, two cars, three.
He's losing time.
He's lost position, the points are draining away.
Time to leave before the rush hour starts.

*Stephen Tuffnell*

## FEEL FREE

The prospective tenant looked for years for a suitable place.
On finding a house which appeared to be furnished and
Decorated solely for children, she quickly took the room being offered.
When the live-in landlord explained the house rule,
'Feel free,' she went happily to her room and cried.

*Millicent Coleman*

## LOCKED IN

Like a bird entrapped in a room fighting for its survival.
Terrified as one tries to set him free, only to fly towards the light
Hitting his head against the windowpane in an effort to escape.
In these moments of panic doctor and patient share a state of confusion.

*Gladys C'Ailceta*

## SNOW WHITE AND THE SEVEN DWARVES

Once upon a time there lived a young lady called Snow White and she lived in a cottage with seven dwarf rabbits, whose names were Bashful, Dopey, Happy, Grumpy, Sneezy, Sleepy and Doc, and they had won many prizes and rosettes.

Now, Snow White's evil step-mother (who just happened to be a witch), also showed rabbits, but she didn't win much.

She had a magic mirror and would always ask it who would win and it always said 'Snow White'. This displeased the witch and she decided to do something about her.

There was a big show coming up and, the day before it, the witch disguised herself as a kind, old lady selling vegetables.

She stopped at Snow White's cottage and persuaded her to buy some lovely cabbages and carrots. But, unbeknown to Snow White, the carrots were dosed with a powerful sleeping potion the witch had concocted. It wouldn't harm her, just make sure she wouldn't be at the show.

But, unbeknown to the witch, Snow White intended to give the vegetables to her prize-winning Dwarves.

Imagine her horror, when, the next morning, five of her seven dwarves were dopey! and sleepy! - including her star rabbit for the show.

What was she to do?

Well, she took one of the other two that were alright and, that night, when she added yet another trophy to her collection she was very happy! but the witch was mightily grumpy!

*Vanessa Bell*

## CINDERELLA

Once upon a time a girl called Cinderella
Had two beautiful sisters
Who were members of a pop group.
Cinderella could not sing
But she was a very good dancer.
The three of them were happy
And together took great delight
In doing housework in their spare time.
One day Cinderella was invited to a disco
And was very excited.
He sisters helped her prepare
And one gave her a mobile phone
So that she could order a new dress from a boutique.
When it arrived it was a beautiful colour,
Rich golden, like a pumpkin.
On the evening of the disco
Her mother reminded her
That the last bus home was at midnight
And if she missed it she would require a taxi.
The disco went well and Cinderella enjoyed herself.
Finally it was time to go and she remembered
That she had to hurry to the bus stop.
In her haste she tripped and a strap on one of her shoes broke.
Poor Cinderella was in rather a panic,
Fortunately a handsome gentleman noticed her plight
And came to her aid.
He was able to repair her shoe
And then offered to give her a lift home
As he lived in the same area.
Cinderella was grateful and when they went outside
She saw that an open topped convertible was parked nearby.

Very soon she was home again and arranged to meet
The good looking man with the convertible next day for coffee.
As time passed away they both went to lots of discos together
And lived happily ever after.

*A H Thomson*

## ONCE UPON A TIME

Once upon a time there were three piglets who ran away from home. It was too dangerous to stay there because the slaughter man was due to visit the farm. So they set off for the hills to hide.

That night they huddled together in a small wood. But they were so cold that the next morning they decided to build themselves a house. All day they worked building a house of straw, it was snug and warm, but that night a hurricane blew through the woods and the piglets clung together as their home collapsed around them.

Shivering the piglets set to work and built themselves a house of sticks. They were just settling down for the night when they heard a noise outside.

The oldest piglet peeped out. There were deer and sheep dashing through the woods.
'The slaughter mans' coming,' called a large stag trying to hide his antlers behind a tree.
'He thinks we're all sick, and he's coming to put us out of our misery.'
'Are you sick?' asked the piglet.
'No' said the stag.
'Follow me' called a sheep as it hurried by. 'Quick all of you.'
The piglets, and the other animals followed the sheep to a deserted farmyard high on the hillside.
'We can hide here,' said the sheep.

The animals hid in the farmyard for a year until the slaughter man left the land. By that time they were such firm friends that they stayed together forever.

*Pat Rissen*

## DARK SHADOW MAN

Run, run,
As fast as you can,
Or I'll catch you
Said the dark shadow man
Hide, hide
As well as you can,
Or I'll see you
Said the dark shadow man
Sleep, sleep,
As long as you can,
And I'll wait till morning
Said the dark shadow man.

*S A Ward*

# WEIRD DREAM

I had the weirdest dream last night,
That I was being chased,
Through lots of empty dark corridors,
And down some stairs I raced.

I ran into an empty room,
- On the windows there were bars,
By the window stood a table,
- On it a large glass vase.

The vase was made of white smoked glass,
With flowers of bright blue,
Too nice to throw at the window,
- But that's what I had to do.

Outside there was a courtyard,
With many piles of straw,
Cobbled stones instead of roads,
And knockers on the doors.

I smashed the window with the vase,
And shouted out for help,
Out there a woman sat spinning,
As a dog began to yelp.

She looked up from her spinning wheel,
- Her hair shone in the sun,
She totally ignored my pleas,
- Then the dream was gone.

*Joyce Clegg*

## My Rainbow's End

The rain clouds cleared, the sun came out,
A rainbow shone so bright,
A multi-coloured bridge, aglow,
As if with inner light.

Its beauty beckoned me to come,
It seemed just like a friend,
With open arms it led on,
To reach its rainbow's end.

I walked through fields, I climbed the hills,
Valleys deep I crossed,
Swam rivers wide, o'er mountain high,
Never getting lost.

Always in sight, but out of reach,
So close, but yet so far,
Tempting, taunting, teasing me,
Just like a guiding star.

Nearly there, I see a field,
Its centre shining gold,
I forge ahead, through hedges high,
Its treasure soon to hold.

Battle scarred, bruised and weak,
Exhausted, weary man,
At last I reach my rainbow's end,
And find, *a pot of jam!*

**Jim Sargant**

# FROZEN IN A SCREAM

They told me He was coming,
They all watched; eyes of false fear.
They told me He returned for me,
Made me believe Him near.

They watched me as I breathed,
As mortality reigned true,
And reminders of the future
Came ever crashing through.

For life and for the telling
My heart did fear to say,
But to you I turned in honesty
To see you turn away.

I thought that you had wishes
To hear those words you speak,
But your expression bore betrayal;
Your honesty was weak.

You laughed into my tears,
The fright my eyes did bleed,
And told me it was all untrue,
And never meant to be.

And smiling you did venture
To caress my broken dream,
But all in you I once held sacred
Was frozen in a scream.

*Helen Marshall*

## ANGLE AND SAXON'S PART IN BRITANNIA'S HISTORY

Angle researched his family tree. Angle 1st married Saxon. They were invaders from Europe. Romans had invaded Britannia's people earlier and Vikings came later. Angle 1st and Saxon's descendants had married descendants of those here before and after. Angle was not who he thought he was.

*Rob Thornhill*

## THERE HAS TO BE AN EASIER WAY

Snaking round endless alleys, empty
headed notions, brings daydreams.
   Bobbing hither and dither, options
considered, choices made.
   Humed a red decision, mindless
confusion, fluorescent lights, swaying
bright signs.
   Unfamiliar faces, isolation
among mayhem.
   Screaming children, arguing
parents,
   All manner of humanity
gobbled together.
   That's fifty-two pounds eighty
         Madam.

*Ann Hathaway*

## MARA

Walking the dog one day, a young man came across a beautiful girl playing a violin. Her name was Mara and she said she would play for him provided he closed his eyes. Alas! He peeped and she was gone forever and only the violin and bow remained.

*Rebecca Osborne*

## SILENCE IS OFTEN THE TRUTH

They all sat with one thing in mind, who did it?
They needed the truth, but it wasn't forthcoming.
No one dare speak
All involved just looking at each other, wondering.
Suddenly, silence was broken, silence had been the key
The truth had been found through the silence held.

*Pauline Porteous*

## OLD DAN'S HOUSE

The rain was pelting down; we saw the house.
The door was ajar; we went in.
The old man stood near the fire, smoking his pipe.
'You can stay,' he said.
'Good morning!' greeted the woman.
Staring, we began, 'The old man didn't say . . .'
She gasped, 'What old man?'

*Licia Johnston*

## STRUGGLE FOR FREEDOM

I watched, helpless, as the struggle began. The shaking and twisting, splitting and tearing, the belly swelling and blood pumping was frightening. I held my breath for what seemed like hours. Suddenly, my heart leapt for joy as the beautiful butterfly rose on flapping wings, and finally soared to freedom.

*Julie Wright*

## JACK AND JILL THE BUILDERS

Jack and Jill walked up the long, trailing winding road.

They carried a bucket up to the builders who were building them a lovely new house . . .

The builders were very glad to see them for they knew they could depend on them to do a few little tasks which would speed them up, bringing tea time a little earlier.

Jill carried lots of water over to Jack in a little pail.

Jack was very busy. He felt like a real man - a builder - whistling and working away - mixing his cement.

Up Jack got onto the scaffolding, reaching up his buckets of water. Then suddenly - *bang!* and down fell Jack.

Jill said, 'Jack I see a scratch on your head. I think you have cracked it.' Then Jill she did a wobble and there they were, both lying at the foot of the tree. Jack with a crack on his crown and Jill with a bump like an apple on her arm.

Up Jack got holding his head in place and trotted off with Jill at his heels, holding onto the apple on her arm.

They ran as fast as they could until they came to the nurse's house.

The nurse glued Jack's head so well together that the crack could not be seen anymore.

She then bandaged the big red apple on Jill's arm so that it could not roll away.

Back they both went to the new house to see the garden full of lovely flowers.

*Elizabeth Jones*

## MALAISE IN CUMBERLAND SEEN THROUGH THE RAVENGLASS

*The poem is a parady of Lewis Carroll's nonsense verse
'Jabberwocky' which he included in Alice's Adventures
Through The Looking Glass. This version makes use of
over 70 Cumbrian place names in the title and text shown
here in italic type face*

'Twas *Bleakrigg* as the *Martindales*
Did *Whale* through all the *Sellafields*
Quite *Strickland* were the *Borrowdales*
Their *Ewes closed* in their *Stonefold Fields.*

*Wrynosed* and *'Pity Me'* they cried:
'Beware the *Cockermouth* my son!
With *Mallerstang*, its lips all wet;
Beware that *Blencow* beast and shun
Its *Skinburness* and *Burnmoor* jet!'

But *Salkeld's* son, so *Bolton* brave
In *Baysbrown Rigg* and *Gelt Dunmail,*
*Gosforth* his *Sharp Edge* sword in hand:
Though *Seldon Seen* in *Eskdale Green,*
*Langdale* the *Foulsyke* foe he sought;
Then left his *Drumleaning,*
His *Steel Pike* at hand,
And *Grasmered* he 'neath the *Appleby* tree
To dream of *Mary Port.*

Till as in *Ulpha* thought and state,
His *Bridekirk* mood was fast *Dockrayed;*
The *Cockermough* with *Burgh Redmain*
Did *Lamplugh* through the *Waberthwaite!*

Once, twice and thrice! Through grey *Seascales*
The *Silloth* sword did *Hackthorpe Shap!*
He left it dead with *Raughtenhead*
And a *Sceughmired Saddleback.*

'Great *Salkeld*'*!* quoth sweet *Mary Port,*
All *Wiggonby* and *Drigg* delight!
'The *Cockermouth* is *Mellerstain,*
*Howe Brandethly* and bravely fought!'
'Come *Armathwaite Close,* my *Darling, Howe*
My *Aikton Hartside* is distraught.'
'My *Blennerhasset!* My *Dearham* heart!'
He *Croglined, Rosley* overwrought.

From the *Wedholme Flow* to
*Castlestead's Great Gables* high,
Did *Mary Port,* no *Maiden Moor;*
*Motherby* young *Kidson Howe?*
With *Dancing Gate* on the *Whitehall floor!*

'Good *Riddings* to the *Cockermouth!'*
Was *Calbecked* through the *Cardewlees,*
All *Hartsopped* were the *Martindales,*
Now *Snittlegarthed* in *Holmes* of ease.

**John Rowland Parker**

## THE TAIL OF THE HAIRLESS KIDOS

Once upon a time, technology overflowed with ideas, that boggled the mind of certain individuals to such an extent that they bubbled over with excitement!

Faces were seen on the computer screen, that opened up all sorts of malfunction, the media became delirious to say the least.

Every computer started to speak its mind, calling their owners, every insulting word one could imagine. It became indiscreet, the language spoken, even people's minds began to grovel and worship their computer as a living god!

One day the electricity failed and their computers went quite dead, all over the world.

People muttered in soft unrecognisable words, sitting on their computer chairs and wringing their hands.

In the meantime, the faces that had been seen on their computer screen were busy making hay! Their home was in outer space, millions of miles away from Earth, it did not stop them gurgling with fruitful laughter.

The best of the world's electricians busied themselves and again managed to get each computer working.

The cosmonauts circling over our planet, heard the muffled cries of the relief of the media. To watch the screen once again gave exceeding pleasure to all and sundry.

The computer faces were greener than ever, they seemed to appear with an odd smile on their faces, before they disappeared.

Computers became quite uncontrollable, making dots, dashes with striped star images, even when the screen appeared blank!

To begin and end all, the computers amazed all. They sputum forth hairless kidos!

*Alma Montgomery Frank*

## THE SWORD OF COURAGE

It was midnight in the forest. The candlelights flickered in the big stone castle across the lake. The campers put their fires out and sat watching the lake. The legend had it that at midnight, on a certain day, a sword would be seen rising from these deep dark waters.

With their modern day minds crammed full of doubt and disbelief, they sat cramming their mouths too with snacks as the watch took place.

There was a horse that regularly foraged for food in the forest. As he trampled through the bushes all eyes were turned from the lake. The campers, greedy for action, looked to discern the source of the commotion behind them.

The white, ghostly-looking figure of the horse caused them to cower and
and move back. Only one moved stealthily toward the figure genuinely wishing to discern the truth.

Seeing it was a horse he turned, ready to tell the others. But as he faced them and the lake the sword appeared. His expression was one of bewilderment, shock and wonder. The campers surmised this was because of the ghostly figure and ran.

The lone seeker of the truth stood transfixed. He was smitten in his heart by the sight of the sword he knew he'd seen.

Nobody would, afterwards, believe him. Yet from that day on his life became more enriched and wonderful than ever, as he carried the sword of courage in his heart.

*Lorenza Cangiano*

## BROADWAY MAGDALENE

It was my last night in Herald Square.
In passing . . . she looked at me.
Her dress was so tight, I was so aware
As that movement in a moment surreal,
Skipped by. A golden armband sparkled.
As if to complement; this glowing twirl,
Turned her perfumed body and charming,
Took my arm to walk with me awhile . . .
From such teeth of pearl seductive, she
So calmly smiled her many reasons but
Within . . . she *was* good, you understand,
Though her chatter exposed liaisons in
Love triangles which suited her, *so far.*
In her mind, she had yet to taste . . .
A better wine but a better life seemed
Hard to find. Hedonism's casks were fine.
'What time was it?' she asked aside, 'Oh,
Must go . . . see you around sometime, bye!'
'So long' I beamed, as she left me there,
I had to let her go, albeit unwillingly,
Being a 'Brit' I wasn't used to it.
She was altogether in her prime, happy,
Living that wild and naughty time.
Sweet she was, a girl I met in the night.
A tricky bet for me, you see, on a flight.
I think she came from the ghettos . . .
All black stockings and stilettos.
'How are you doin? . . . You're new here,'
Ah! but that's life, what a place America.

She thought I was sad, naive but 'not bad'
I had to leave then, you know how it is,
I wrote this poem for my 'vice' girl . . .
'She was a very nice girl . . . not just,
Here to tease us . . . to me she seemed
More like . . . Magdalene . . . with Jesus . . .'

***Roger Mosedale***

## THE SLEEPING BEAUTY

Once upon a time, there lived a young woman called Krystal. She was the laziest, good for nothing girl there ever was. Krystal spent her days watching TV in bed and having long lie-ins. Her father grew bored of tidying her room because Krystal never cleared anything away. So he left her room, which quickly grew into an utter mess, full of rubbish and rotting food.

Krystal never got out of bed, unless she could help it. She loved watching her favourite show, 'Boo! Got you!' where the host, Sam Peters, barged in on people and gave them a shock. It just so happened that the show came to Krystal's town, and when the producers heard about her, they decided to pay her a visit.

As they tried to get to her room, the crew had to literally fight their way through all the plates, pizza boxes and other rubbish Krystal had built up. Finally Sam got into her room, where she lay dozing. Silently he made his way over, then yelled his famous catchphrase, 'Boo! Got you!'

Krystal woke up with a start, saw the hunk leaning over her and decided that bed was worth getting out of! The producers decided to keep her on the show and she became a presenter with Sam.

She soon became a world famous star, and in true celebrity fashion, married Sam in a glitzy wedding and they all lived happily ever after.

*Lucy Webb*

## THREE BAGS LATER . . .

Barnabas Black Sheep was lost. He'd been happily scrunching the lush grass, not realising that he'd wandered onto the road till a car pulled up near him. A man and woman got out.

'Let's get you back to the field.' The man got hold of the sheep but the woman stopped him.

'What lovely wool it's got. I could spin some for your new jumper.' She produced a pair of clippers and collected a bag full of wool leaving a huge bare patch on Barnabas' back. They forgot about putting him back in the field.

Presently a motorbike came along.

The lady rider surveyed the sheep in a business-like manner.

'Well, I never saw a half-sheared sheep before. I'd better tidy you up.' Soon she too, had filled a bag with Barnabas' lovely black wool.

Barnabas was bleating pitifully when a bicycle bell rang and up rode a schoolboy. He looked at Barnabas and burst out laughing. He was on his way to cut his grandmother's hedge. He pulled a pair of shears from his saddlebag.

Clip, clip, clip. Another bag of black wool. Barnabas was now in a very sorry state. What *would* the farmer say?

He slunk into a ditch to hide and there the farmer eventually found him.

'That'll teach you to wander off,' he chuckled, hauling Barnabas into the truck. Barnabas was so pleased to be found that he didn't even say 'baa'.

But he never ventured onto the road again.

*Patricia Batstone*

## UP AND FALL

Once upon a time
there lived in a
bungalow, a tall lady
called Sophie Jones
who had very long hair.

As her home needed
exterior decoration,
Sophie decided to go
out and buy a ladder
from B & B Barbeque.

As she climbed up, the
ladder fell down and
she got stuck on the
roof.

Luckily Mr Edward
from Buckingham Road
was passing by, he
spotted Ms Jones stuck
on the roof. Deciding
to help her, he picked
up the ladder and
started climbing up.

Relieved, Sophie stared
watching Mr Edward
coming up, she had just
about managed to slip
safely down on to the
balcony, however the
balcony door was
locked. She was aware
of unwanted intruders.

Suddenly she saw that
Mr Edward was
struggling on the ladder
halfway, as a step had
broken. Seeing no
other alternative she
decided to let down her
hair and help him
climb up.

So it ended with them
rescuing each other.

Mr Edward said, 'I'm
so sorry to have hurt
your head madam.'
Sophie replied
'No, not at all sir, it
was kind of you though
to come up as I could
have climbed down
instead.' Edward
replied:
'No, no madam that
would not have been a
gentleman's job.'
Sophie asked, 'But why
didn't you use the
stairs, sir?'
'Have you forgotten
madam, a bungalow
doesn't have stairs.'
They both laughed.

Later on that month
they got married and
lived happily ever
after.

*Shahmima Khanom*

## BUTTERFLY BALLET

Dancing over the garden
In your orange shoes,
Laughing on the grasses,
Playing on the dews.

Stealing sunbeam kisses,
Running in the rain,
Flying black-jewelled flowers
In a country lane.

Colours of the rainbow
In your pretty wings,
Ballet of the butterfly
As the summer sings.

*Marion Schoeberlein*

## ALAS POOR YORICK

Alas poor Yorick I knew him well
But I didn't push him down the well
When I saw Yorick last
He was stood on the side
Having a crafty slash
Then I heard a mighty splash
And when I looked round
Alas poor Yorick could not be found
Then I heard a moaning sound
Coming from the bottom of the well
For poor Yorick I was afraid and ran to his aid
But as I did I slipped and slid
And knocked the bucket on his head
And now alas poor Yorick is *dead*

**Philip Robertson**

## 'PAGING DOCTOR HACKENSACK'

Hackensack failed his medical exams, and had a long-standing grudge against the Mid Town Hospital.

Mid Town Hospital was very old, and like every similar building, had a closed down, 'no go' area, where all old junk was dumped.

Stuff like Zimmer frames, old operating tables, scalpels, and many rusty lockers, broken junk, and hospital garbage.

This section attracted those 'Looney Tunes' like Hackensack, who prowled the unused wards wearing stolen hospital white coats.

They lived in a fantasy world where they were qualified medics.

The police knew about this closed down area, and wisely, chose to ignore its existence, after a police officer was found dead from a badly botched operation carried out by one of the 'Looney Tunes', who was never discovered.

Hackensack found out who it was, when one dark night, he entered through a broken window, and was laid low by someone wielding a piece of lead pipe. When he woke up he was strapped to an operating table.
'Don't worry' said a soothing voice, 'you know I am the Surgeon General.'

Before Hackensack could scream, or try to struggle free from his restraints, the rusty scalpel was already flashing downwards . . .

*Gordon Bannister*

## HIS BLACKEST NIGHTMARE

He lay there.

Motionless.

His arms locked around the headless corpse leaking blood over his smooth skin, soaking the floor around them both; warming his cold flesh even as the life drained from his lover's remains.

He knew he had been powerless to do anything.

His heart banged deafeningly in his chest, almost choking him with its force. He felt sure the creature must hear it and would soon return to end him too.

The rasp of the creature's tail on the soft carpet, its heavy laboured breathing, were the only sounds outside himself that were discernible in the still night. These sounds grew fainter as it disappeared from the scene of its crime.

He had created it. He had given it life.

It had been born from the darkest recesses of his mind; made corporeal by his most secret desires and fantasies; taken shape from his blackest nightmare.

He had awoken just in time to see his lover's head disappear down the maw of the monster. And he had done nothing; had wanted to do nothing.

Now as the enormity of what had befallen him finally hit home, the unremitting loneliness that was now his only future, a tiny sob escaped from his throat . . .

Then silence.

Then . . .

He couldn't bring himself to move even as the head of the creature reappeared at the door, obsidian eyes and skewer teeth glinting in the sensual moonlight . . .

*John Harold*

## THE WOOD FOLK

Have you heard the joyful tinkle of the fairies down the glen?
Have you seen the darting twinkle when they moved among the men?
It was when the dawn was scented, in the golden days when
Pollution wasn't invented, the woods were lovely then!
Every flower was respected and the grass was soft and green,
All the blossoms were inspected by the bees in yellow sheen,
From the meadows elves would gather and would hold, a picnic treat,
In the pathways of the forest you'd see marks of elfin feet;
Girls and boys could go and greet them, 'twas perchance a place
                                                    to dream.
The wood folk would come to meet them on a rainbow's silver beam,
They would teach them nature's lore and the secrets of the glen,
But all this was long before all the woods were raped by men.
You won't hear the fairies singing if you walk the woods at night,
You won't hear the elf bells ringing or observe their flitting light,
Good King Pan won't play his flute, and the birds are also mute,
They've all gone, it's just too late, and they've left us to our fate.

*Emmanuel Petrakis*

## JACK AND THE CARPORT

Once upon a time Little Jack and Mini his mum lived along from the back of beyond, they'd lost all their money on the stock market, now making a living, buying and selling cars.

Jack climbed high up the Cadilac stack to the Mondeo on top, collecting its radiator. Noticing the staircase leading from the Silver Cloud on the adjacent stack. Jack drops the radiator on a rope with a note telling Mini he was climbing the staircase.

Soon up the stairs to a plateau which contained a large mansion. Jack was scared when a giant bellowed out 'Fiesta, Sierra, Jenson and Allegro, by whose authority do you go?'

Jack thinking on his feet called, 'I want my rent money, which is a million, plus higher purchase and VAT.'
'What pray are they?' asks the giant.
'Higher purchase is calculated on the height you're at, VAT is Vauxhall added tax because you drive a Vauxhall. So it's one and a half million cash please,' boldly Jack states.

'I know you have the money, your cousin the Golly Green Giant has been charging the kids to cross the road for years.' The giant agrees to pay but grumbles that he won't have a Sou-baru left.
'Tough' says Jack as he prepares to leave.

Jack returns to Mini with sacks of cash, 'We're rich beyond our dreams, the giant's paid his rent in full, he now knows who calls the tune. Any trouble from him and I'll set my Land Rovers on him.'

*P J Littlefield*

## THREE LITTLE PIGS

Once upon a time lived three little pigs
who lived in a splendid sty.
Tho' the farmer was kind, he had
pork on his mind
and fattened them up, to die.

But the three little pigs had minds of
their own
and decided to do a runner.
On the day they left, the sky was blue and
the day had never been sunnier.

Deciding perhaps that three was a crowd
and longing for some freedom,
they made their way to a building site
and proceeded to do some building.

The first little pig built his house of straw,
His dad had been a thatcher,
It didn't stand up to a gust of wind
and ended in disaster.

The second little pig chose to build with wood,
He had never heard of woodworm,
and slow but sure the house fell down
leaving another little piggy homeless.

Now the third little piggy was nobody's fool,
He was always up to tricks.
In the middle of the night by pale moonlight
he built his house with bricks.

When Mr Wolf came he couldn't get in,
The windows and doors were barred.
There wasn't even a chimney pot,
Central heating had been installed.

So to this day lives piggy three in his house he
built of bricks
with all mod cons and en-suite rooms,
making piggies one and two feel sick.

*Winifred Lund*

## WILF AND THE THREE POGS

It could be so tiresome battling through the polluted sky. Too many spacecars taking up precious air, but rent was owed, plus the extra kept for himself. Those pogs had to pay up, unless they wanted to live on that awful place called Earth. So, despite his annoyance, Wilf charged on. He soon reached much greener and less congested pastures. There was even the odd flower. He glanced at his side pocket - the bubble zapper was still there. However, those pogs were so timid. Too scared to even open their mouths. You would think he was going to eat them! Mind you, someone had once told him . . . oh, never worry!

Soon he arrived at the space bubble where three frightened pogs lived. He used his ejector seat to exit the car and sauntered (if you can in space), to the transparent door. 'Hand over your money now,' shouted Wilf. No reply. 'Hand over your rent money this instant,' raged Wilf. No reply. 'Hand over the dosh or I'll use my bubble zapper and blow your bubble house away! Down, to that dreaded place Earth!' Wilf bellowed.

A few moments later the door creaked open. The three pogs appeared and said, 'Go away you bully and don't ever come back.' Wilf was so shocked that he accidentally set off his bubble zapper and zapped himself down, down, down to Earth.

The three pogs looked at each other and smiled. Wilf would not bother them again.

*Carolyn Hall*

## ADRIFT

Once upon a time when Fairy and Elf were floating gently on their raft and it was time to paddle into shore, the sea got out of hand as it often does and they were swept out. Fairy got into a fluster and unruffled Elf continued admiring Fairy's ever-changing beauty including many spiritual and intellectual qualities. Elf prevented Fairy from going overboard and after a while they found themselves on a calm sea accepting things philosophically not to say joyfully, at least in the case of Elf.

At last they were washed up on to the shores of a beautiful deserted tropical island with palm trees to provide shade for Fairy. They felt free at last and merged into ElFairy in the warm sand. When they awoke a wonderful crystal castle had sprung up around them. The crystal took on one or some or all of the rainbow colours of Fairy's eyes, depending on her thoughts and moods, and ElFairy lived there happily ever after.

*Elaine Harris*

## THE THREE LITTLE PIGS

Once upon a time piggy no 1 said, 'I can't find my new CD - 'slike looking for a needle in a haystack!'
Piggy 2 said . . . 'But we are living in a haystack!'
Piggy 1 said, 'Oh, yes . . . I forgot.'

One day when the 3 little pigs were out, a big bad wolf property developer blew up their place because he wanted the site to build a supermarket. The 3 little pigs being 3 little pigs couldn't do anything except start again. They moved to the sticks and built a house . . . from sticks.

'Strewth! . . . it looks like a real log-cabin!' said piggy 3.
'That's because . . . it *is* a log-cabin' said Piggy 1.
They had a TV interior designer in to Queen Anne their living room.

While the 3 little pigs were on holiday the big bad wolf property developer . . . decided he wanted that site for a Health Farm, and blew up the house and the little pigs being little pigs, couldn't do anything except start from scratch and this time built a beautiful red-brick bungalow in the middle of nowhere.

The big bad wolf property developer thought he might like their place to build a Hotel and tried to blow it up . . . but there were no explosives strong enough and so he gave in. And the 3 happy little pigs had someone in to give their house the Minimalist Look.

*Lorna Liffen*

## MODERN DAY FAIRY TALE

'you're concerned about your mother?'
'Yes.'
'She's in debt?'
'Yes.'
'Fear not your grandmother will help.'

How could this Psychic or 'Spookie' know so much? How could Nana help Mum? It was impossible, Nana had passed away last year. A few days later I called at Mum's.
'Honey, you know I need a new winter coat?' Mum started.
'Well I've got your Nan's old fur coat upstairs in the wardrobe. You know how hopeless I am at sewing, could you help me take it up and in?'
'Alright Mum, get it down, let's see what we have to do.'

I measured her up. As we laid the coat flat there was a bump which wasn't apparent as it hung in the closet. We looked at each other puzzled and checked the pockets. It was in the lining. I swiftly unpicked the lining and a large manila envelope fell out. Hardly daring to breathe my nerveless fingers struggled to open it. Fifteen hundred pounds in fifties! What a Godsend! We were both in tears as we hugged, Mum tearful and offering me half. God bless her!

Good old Nana! She had not been bothering with the bank since it relocated several miles away. She was also terrified of being burgled. Perhaps that's why she hid it there. Well, whatever, it would help Mum out of the jam. What about the 'Spook', had Nana told him? Well, I really believe she did.

*S Murphy*

## BUTTONS

Buttons, sighed loudly, what a way to spend a Saturday night.
All his mates would be down at the pub.
And what was he doing? Nothing! It was his own fault, he could have gone with Cinderella, she had asked him.
He had said no because there was football on the telly, or there should have been. To his dismay he found that it had been cancelled.

'What's the matter with you?'
Cindi's fairy godmother stood by his side impatiently tapping one size ten shoe.
Buttons explained about the cancelled football match.
'Do you want to go and see the match?'
'Of course I do but how? I haven't got time to get to the ground and even if I did I haven't got a ticket.'
The godmother gave her wand a little shake.
Magic dust blew into Button's face.
'Careful with that stuff' he sneezed.
'Bring me an old lottery ticket.'
Button's searched inside his pockets and pulled out a tattered ticket.
She zapped it with her wand, a season ticket appeared.
She swirled her wand over his head, his dark green uniform disappeared, replaced by a football strip in his team's colours;
Buttons was delighted, then frowned.
'Now what's the matter?' the godmother was getting impatient.
'How am I going to get there? The game starts soon.'

Her broom hovered inches from the floor, nimbly she jumped onto it.
'Come on then,' she urged, 'I might even get that nice David Beckham's autograph.'

*Jacky Stevens*

## THREE DUCKS

Once upon a time . . .

Three ducks swam on the village pond, during a thunderstorm the ducks dived under the shelter of the magic rock. There they changed into three bears, where to their amazement they discovered another world of little people. It was a magical place, snails grew on trees like large lollipops. Spaghetti and porridge hung like drooping branches from all the shrubs. Fish swam in backward races and jumped over hoops left on the bed of water lilies. Elves chased pixies and leapt over frogs resting on the cold stones.

It was a land of magic play. Everyone was so kind and happy and no one went short of food. When they became hungry they would rub the magical rock. It would spin round three times then a window would open and a voice called out, 'Place your order' just like at Donald Mac's. Everything was free, they did not need money there.

The three bears got excited when they saw honey dripping all around them, like fountains of pure gold. After a while they tried out all the furniture in a funny little house. In the bedroom they found a little girl asleep on the large water bed. Her name was 'Tiger Lily'. They were amazed at all the things they had seen. By now they were feeling tired so they came up from the pond's bed, instantly changing back into the three ducks. They swam round the pond once more, before settling down to sleep. That night they began to wonder if everything they had done and seen that day had just been a magical, wonderful dream.

*Pamela M Wild*

## THE ESCAPE OF THE PRINCESS

The beautiful princess looked out from the grim castle on a pale moonlight night. She waited until everything was still and quiet, hoping that all the people in the castle were fast asleep, especially her strict father, who never understood her.

She quietly crept down the broad, stone, spiral stairway with her shoes in her hands. She slipped into the utility room, got the can of WD40, shook it, and sprayed the contents on to the lock of the door liberally, and also the key.

She turned the key slowly in the lock of the huge door, sneaked out silently and was free of the interior of the castle. She hurried to the large north gate and climbed over it. She rushed to the edge of the forest, even though she was early for her tryst with her secret lover.

She waited impatiently for the sound of her lover's car. Where was he? Had his car broken down? Did he have a flat tyre? Why didn't she buy a mobile when she saw them at the sale the other day?

At last she heard the sound of a car on the forest road. She saw the headlights - she looked at the registration number - yes it was him. She came out from behind a large Red Wood tree and stood in the silver moonlight. He stopped. She ran to the car and they went off together, far away, into the moonlight.

*Lyn Richard*

## PIED AND RATS OF HAMBLING RAMBLING

Brendan McTavish's piper - lived in the slums, made up of bums, drug dealers, mice and rats.

They used to call him - Pied but he was never that, maybe eccentric, maybe not. However this tale was begun with you being informed by me. How and where and why - *Pied,* rats and slums came to be a fairy tale.

In this century maybe - the 18th? 16th? - No, it was last year. *Pied* lived with his two sisters in Cornwall - now anyone who has been to Cornwall knows him, he sits by the side of Bodmin Moor for hours on end, just piping on a long flute-like pipe his father made for him when he was little. Well he's only 4'5" now and he gave *Pied* lessons on how to get the girls, and a few other things besides, by enthralling people at Carnivals and Fairs, and he did a fair bit of Morris dancing too. He had all the equipment - Tyrrolean hat, knickerbockers, scarf and dirty white shirt, shoes with buckles of course. Well he'd been listening to radio five one day when he heard that a town called Penzance, somewhere the other side of the world, needed a rat catcher, as their own bloke had gone down with the Black Death. Now Pied was very wary what he took on, but decided to go with his two sisters as well.

When they arrived there was this awful smell of drains, but he pressed on and met the Mayor, a nice chap, who told him he'd get him a job on the Council if he got rid of the rats. So he began to pipe along the streets giving the children a bar of Cadbury's between them. About fifty there were, well he drove all the rats into the sea. Then set up a plumbing business and his sisters became nurses, occasionally they all sat in Bodmin. *Pied* piped and his sisters nursed a grievance.

*Albert Boddison*

# REALITY OF A FAIRY TALE

Light flooded into the twins' bedroom, creating mystical
Patterns, on the wall, and ceiling.
The light grew brighter, and brighter, the patterns became more
Pronounced, and began to materialise into
Realistic shapes.

Figures of people, shelters for protection, animals, trees,
Stars began appearing, high on the ceiling.
The twins whispered to each other. Wondering what was
Going to happen.

The breeze from their whisper, caused a murmur of movement,
Amongst the scene, on the wall and ceiling,
As if the wind had risen.
Slowly the figures, with the animals, began moving
Across the wall, towards the shelters.

The twins hardly believing what they were seeing,
Everything seemed so exciting.
As they watched, the stars started descending from
The ceiling, onto the surface, where upon the figures,
And animals, climbed on board the stars, and began
Floating around the room, above the heads of the twins.

The figures waved to the children, the animals also
Sent a greeting of pleasure.
Slowly circling the bedroom, they formed a ring of
Wonder, and mystery. Enjoying this special moment,
Of make-believe.
Which was now creating the shape of a heart,
Bestowing warmth, and love upon the twins.

For a while the symbol of love hovered, filling the
Room with a comforting, soothing feeling.
Leaping from their beds, the twins knelt beside them,
Closing their eyes, and putting their hands together,
They thanked God,
For reminding them to say their prayers . . .

*Lorna Tippett*

## I Don't Believe In Santa Claus

Once upon a time there were seven year old twins Simon and Peter.
Peter believed in Santa Claus but Simon did not. In fact his mummy and
daddy had a job to get Simon to hang his stocking up on Christmas Eve.
Finally he did and the boys eventually went to sleep.

In the middle of the night Simon woke up. He looked around and
realised he was not in his own bedroom. Apart from the beds, there was
no furniture in it at all. Simon jumped out of bed and looked out of the
window and found it was not the garden and very snowy.

'Wake up Peter, wake up!'

'What's up?' asked Peter wiping his eyes, 'has Santa come?'

'No, we are not at home.' Simon stuttered.

'We must be!'

Peter got out of bed and looked out of the window.

'But where are we?'

'And how did we get here?' added Simon.

'I don't know but there is a door there, should we go through it?'
suggested Peter.

'We might get into trouble' said Simon.

'Coward' snarled Peter, slowly opening the door.

Then they saw a giant room full of coloured toys.

'Come on Simon, I'm going to ride that bike.'

Soon both boys were enjoying riding bikes and scooters and banging
tambourines.

'Ho! Ho! Ho!'

'We like your toys' stammered Simon.

'Good! Merry Christmas.'

'He does not believe in you' laughed Peter.

'Do you now?' asked Santa.

'I certainly do!'

*Jenny Bosworth*

## SINDRELLA

Sindrella was a Spanish au pair. However, when she came to England she just had to look after two fat ugly old sisters. No kids! She had all the hardest work to do for Fanny and Freda who gave her no money and fed her on scraps. It was lucky for them that Sindrella didn't report them to the Social Services.

There was to be a right rave-up at the Palais and Fanny and Freda got invites.

Everyone was after the MP for Feather Frumpington. He was a smasher and knew how to pull strings regarding reducing Council Tax.

Fanny and Freda went to the rave-up dressed to the nines but poor Sindrella not only spoke very little English but had no suitable clothes. She turned up in jeans, T-shirt and trainers.

The MP, Philip Freebody, was much sought after and knew how to swing his hips.

When Sindrella went to the ladies she left a trainer behind. They weren't hers. Philip picked it up. Then nature called. As he vacated the gents he saw Sindrella limping with her one trainer.

'You should buy trainers that fit,' he teased.
'I 'ave no monnee,' wailed Sindrella. 'I work - I get no pay!'
'We'll have to look into this,' said Philip. 'I'm an MP.'
'Money Person?'
'Sort of.'

Philip not only sorted out the scheming sisters but married the lovely Sindrella to boot.

It goes to show!

*Ruth Daviat*

# SUBMISSIONS INVITED
*SOMETHING FOR EVERYONE*

**POETRY NOW 2001** - Any subject,
any style, any time.

**WOMENSWORDS 2001** - Strictly women,
have your say the female way!

**STRONGWORDS 2001** - Warning!
Age restriction, must be between 16-24,
opinionated and have strong views.
(Not for the faint-hearted)

All poems no longer than 30 lines.
Always welcome! No fee!
Cash Prizes to be won!

Mark your envelope (eg *Poetry Now) 2001*
Send to:
Forward Press Ltd
Remus House, Coltsfoot Drive,
Peterborough, PE2 9JX

**OVER £10,000 POETRY PRIZES
TO BE WON!**

Judging will take place in October 2001